Historiography in the Twentie

Historiography in the Twentieth Century

From Scientific Objectivity to the Postmodern Challenge

WITH A NEW EPILOGUE BY THE AUTHOR

Georg G. Iggers

Wesleyan University Press
Middletown, Connecticut

Published by Wesleyan University Press
Middletown, CT 06459

An expanded English version of the book *Geschichtswissenschaft im 20. Jahrhundert. Ein kritischer Überblick im internationalen Vergleich* (Göttingen, 1993). Published with permission of the German publisher Vandenhoeck & Ruprecht in Göttingen.

Originally produced in 1997 by Wesleyan/University Press of New England, Hanover, NH 03755.

Wesleyan University Press edition including a new epilogue by the author first produced in 2005.

ISBN 0-8195-6766-3
Library of Congress Control Number 2004115137
Printed in the United States of America   5   4   3   2   1

The Library of Congress has cataloged the original edition as follows:

Library of Congress Cataloging-in-Publication Data

Iggers, Georg G.
 [Geschichtswissenschaft im 20. Jahrhundert. English]
 Historiography in the twentieth century : from scientific objectivity to the postmodern challenge / by Georg G. Iggers.
   p.   cm.
 An expanded English version of: Geschichtswissenschaft im 20. Jahrhundert. © 1993.
 Includes bibliographical references and index.
 ISBN 0-8195-5302-6 (cl : alk. paper).
 ISBN 0-8195-6306-4 (pa : alk. paper)
   1. Historiography—History—20th century. 2. History—Philosophy. 3. History—Methodology. I. Title.
 D13.2.I3413   1997
 907'.2-dc20   96-24058

For Wilma

Contents

III. History and the Challenge of Postmodernism

Preface and Acknowledgments

A German version of this book was published in 1993 and in the meantime has been translated into Chinese, Japanese, and Spanish. The German text had its basis in a paper I delivered at a panel discussion in April 1990 at the Philadelphia Philosophy Consortium on "Rationality and History," which dealt with the question of the postmodernist challenge to historical studies. The English version is not a translation of the German but in many ways a different book, the result of additional reading and discussions as well as the critical distance I have gained from the German text in the past three years.

Two observations: Although the book attempts a comparative examination of historical thought that is international in its scope, it restricts itself to languages I can read. Hence the focus is on Great Britain and North America, France and Belgium, German-speaking Central Europe and Italy, with occasional references to Polish and Russian works in translation. But even here, my choice of authors is by necessity highly selective, focusing mainly on historians who exemplify important trends in historical scholarship.

I am very grateful to the students and colleagues who during the past six years permitted me to test my theses and who commented on earlier versions of the manuscript. I am particularly thankful to the members of my seminar at the University of Leipzig who read and commented on a draft of the German manuscript during my guest semester there in the summer of 1992 and to a large number of colleagues and friends on both sides of the Atlantic and in Japan who also read the manuscript and offered critical suggestions, including Werner Berthold, Gerald Diesener, Christoph Dipper, Wolfgang Ernst, Dagmar Friedrich, Akira Hayashima, Wolfgang Hardtwig, Frank Klaar, Wolfgang Küttler, Jonathan Knudsen, Iris Pilling, Lutz Raphael, Anne-Katrin Richter, Hans Schleier, Ulrich Schneckener, Fernando Sánchez Marcos, Christian Simon, B. Stråth, Rudolf von Thadden, Wiebke von Thadden, Edoardo Tortarolo, Johan van der Zande, and Peter Walther. I wish to thank Ottavia Niccoli for her useful suggestions on recent Italian social and cultural history. I found the Max Planck Institute for History in Göttingen a congenial and stimulating place to write the major portions of both the German and the English version. The Institute provided me not only access to an excellent library but also an opportunity to discuss the book with researchers there who read all or large portions of the book, including Hans-Erich Bödeker, Alf Lüdtke, Otto Gerhard Oexle, Jürgen Schlumbohm, and Rudolf Vierhaus. Conversations with Jörn Rüsen, who invited me to a number of colloquia at the Center for Interdisciplinary Studies in Bielefeld, were also valuable. On the German side, Winfried Hellmann at Vandenhoeck & Ruprecht was a superb editor who met with me repeatedly prior to the publication of the German text and offered trenchant criticisms. I am very thankful to Peter Burke who on very short notice read the English manuscript and made valuable suggestions, which I incorporated, and to Albert Cremer and Steffen Kaudelka at the Max Planck Institute and Patrice Veit of the Mission Historique Française en Allemagne for reading the English version of the *Annales* chapter. I would like to thank Karl Sieverling at the Max Planck Institute for his computer assistance. Charles Daniello at Lockwood Library at the State University often provided bibliographical information. I am thankful to my Buffalo assistant Song-Ho Ha for the superb secretarial and scholarly assistance he offered me. The State University of New York at Buffalo was very generous in arranging my teaching schedule to permit me maximum time for my research and writing. The Woodrow Wilson Center provided support for a larger project of which this book was a part, and the Alexander von Humboldt Foundation provided me with the means to spend two half-years in Germany. I am particularly thankful to my wife, Wilma, who carefully read every German and English version for style and logical consistency and prepared a draft translation into English.

G. G. I.

Göttingen
May 1996

Introduction

Over twenty years ago I published a small book about the state
of historical studies in Europe at that time, in which I showed
how the traditional forms of scholarship were replaced by newer
forms of historical research in the social sciences.[1] Historians in
all countries were largely in agreement that research as it had
been practiced internationally since the beginning of historical
studies as a professional discipline in the early nineteenth century corresponded neither to the social nor to the political conditions of the second half of the twentieth century nor to the
demands of a modern science. Meanwhile ideas about history
and historiography have again undergone a profound change.
This volume should therefore not be seen as a continuation
which, so to say, would bring my publication of 1975 up to date.
Instead, it is mainly concerned with a select number of basic
changes in the thinking and in the practice of historians today.
Although there are many continuities with older forms of historical research and historical writing, a basic reorientation has
taken place.

Increasingly in the last twenty years the assumptions upon
which historical research and writing have been based since the
emergence of history as a professional discipline in the nineteenth century have been questioned. Many of these assumptions go back to the beginnings of a continuous tradition of
Western historiography in Classical antiquity. What was new in
the nineteenth century was the professionalization of historical
studies and their concentration at universities and research cen-

ters. Central to the process of professionalization was the firm belief in the scientific status of history. The concept *science* was, to be sure, understood differently by historians than by natural scientists, who sought knowledge in the form of generalizations and abstract laws. For the historians history differed from nature because it dealt with meanings as they expressed themselves in the intentions of the men and women who made history and in the values and mores that gave societies cohesion. History dealt with concrete persons and concrete cultures in time. But the historians shared the optimism of the professionalized sciences generally that methodologically controlled research makes objective knowledge possible. For them as for other scientists truth consisted in the correspondence of knowledge to an objective reality that, for the historian, constituted the past "as it had actually occurred."[2] The self-definition of history as a scientific discipline implied for the work of the historian a sharp division between scientific and literary discourse, between professional historians and amateurs. The historians overlooked the extent to which their research rested on assumptions about the course of history and the structure of society that predetermined the results of their research.

The transformation of history into an institutionalized discipline must not, however, lead us to overlook the continuities with older forms of historical writing. The historiography of the nineteenth century stood in a tradition that went back to the great historians of Classical Greek antiquity. They shared with Thucydides the distinction between myth and truth, and at the same time, despite their stress on the scientific and hence nonrhetorical character of historical writing, proceeded in the classical tradition of historical writing in presupposing that history is always written as a narrative. The problem with historical narrative, however, as Hayden White[3] and other recent theorists of history have pointed out, is that, while it proceeds from empirically validated facts or events, it necessarily requires imaginative steps to place them in a coherent story. Therefore a fictional element enters into all historical discourse.

Hence the break between the "scientific" history of the nineteenth century and the older literary traditions of history was by no means as great as many nineteenth-century historians had

assumed. "Scientific" historical discourse invol\
imagination while the older literary tradition also s
the reconstruction of a real past. The "scientific'
since Leopold von Ranke shared three basic assum\
the literary tradition from Thucydides to Gibbon: (1)
cepted a correspondence theory of truth holding that
portrays people who really existed and actions that reall, .ook
place. (2) They presupposed that human actions mirror the intentions of the actors and that it is the task of the historian to
comprehend these intentions in order to construct a coherent
historical story. (3) They operated with a one-dimensional,
diachronical conception of time, in which later events follow
earlier ones in a coherent sequence. These assumptions of reality, intentionality, and temporal sequence determined the structure of historical writing from Herodotus and Thucydides to
Ranke, and from Ranke well into the twentieth century. Precisely these assumptions have gradually been questioned in
recent historical thought.

I believe we can distinguish two very different orientations
in historical thought in the twentieth century. The first dealt
with the transformation of the kind of narrative, event-oriented
history characteristic of professional historiography in the nineteenth century into social science-oriented forms of historical
research and writing in the twentieth century. Fundamental assumptions of the traditional historiography were challenged,
but the basic assumptions outlined above remained intact. The
various kinds of social science-oriented history spanned the
methodological and ideological spectrum from quantitative sociological and economic approaches and the structuralism of the
Annales-School to Marxist class analysis. In different ways all
these approaches sought to model historical research more
closely after the natural sciences. While traditional historiography had focused on the agency of individuals and on elements
of intentionality that defied reduction to abstract generalization,
the new forms of social science-oriented history emphasized social structures and processes of social change. Nevertheless they
shared two key notions with the older historiography. One was
the affirmation that history dealt with a real subject matter to
which the accounts formulated by historians must correspond.

Admittedly this reality could not be grasped directly but, like all science, must be mediated by the concepts and mental constructs of historians who nonetheless still aimed at objective knowledge. The new social science approaches criticized the older historiography on several counts: They argued that it too narrowly focused on individuals, especially "great men," and events as making up the subject matter of history and that it neglected the broader context in which these operated. In this sense social science approaches, whether Marxist, Parsonian, or Annalist, represented a democratization of history, an inclusion of broader segments of the population, and an extension of the historical perspective from politics to society. They objected to the older approaches, not because they were scientific but because they were not sufficiently so. They challenged one of the basic assumptions of this older approach, namely that history deals with particulars, not generalizations, that its aim is to "understand," not to "explain," and they maintained instead that all sciences, including history, must include causal explanations.

On a second point there was also agreement between the older tradition and the social science approaches. Both operated with a notion of unilinear time, with the conception that there was continuity and direction in history, that in fact there was such a thing as *history* in contrast to a multiplicity of histories. This conception of history took a different form in the older conventional historiography than in the later social science approaches. Ranke had rejected the notion of a philosophy of history that presupposed a scheme of universal history, but nevertheless presupposed that history possessed an inner coherence and development,[4] and assigned a privileged position to the history of the West. Social science historians tended to believe that there at least the history of the modern age moved in a clear direction. While few would accept an idea of progress that endowed this direction with a beneficial character, most operated with a notion of "modernization" or progressive "rationalization" that endowed historical development with coherence. Here too the history of the modern Western world had a privileged status. The history of the world coincided with Westernization.

These assumptions have been increasingly challenged in philosophic thought since the late nineteenth century. It is, however, only in the last quarter century that the doubts this challenge has produced have seriously affected the work of historians. This reorientation of historical thought reflected fundamental changes in society and culture. In a sense the paradigm of professional historiography initiated by Ranke had already been out of tune with the social and political realities of the time when it became the standard for historical studies universally. Ranke was very much a child of the age of restoration that followed the French Revolution and the Napoleonic Era. His concept of the state rested on the political realities of pre-1848 Prussia, prior to the establishment of representative institutions and prior to industrialization with its social concomitants. Hence the emphasis on the primacy of politics relatively isolated from economic or social forces and the almost exclusive reliance on official documents of state. By the time in the late nineteenth century when this paradigm became the model for professional historiography in France,[5] the United States,[6] and elsewhere, the social and political conditions it presupposed had already been fundamentally transformed.

By the turn of the century, historians in France, Belgium, the United States, Scandinavia, and even Germany began to criticize the Rankean paradigm and to call for a history that accounted for social and economic factors.[7] Such a history necessarily had to turn away from a concentration on events and individual leading personalities to focus on the social conditions in which these existed. Democratization and the emergence of a mass society also called for a historiography that took into account the role of broader segments of the population and the conditions under which they lived. Thus from different perspectives New Historians in the United States, the circle around Henri Berr in France and Henri Pirenne[8] in Belgium, and Marxists generally in Continental Europe turned to their particular conceptions of social science as integral to the work of the historians. While conventional forms of political and diplomatic history dominated in the profession until well after 1945, increasing attention was given to social history. Particularly after 1945 the systematic social sciences began to play an increasingly important role in the work of historians. It is this transformation that my book of twenty years ago portrayed.

Yet the optimism regarding the nature and direction of the modern world on which social science history rested was profoundly shaken by fundamental changes in the structure of social existence in a late industrial world. Social science-oriented historians had conceived the modern world more dynamically than did the Rankean school. They envisaged continuous economic growth and the application of scientific rationality to the ordering of society as positive values that defined modern existence.

Already in the second half of the nineteenth century these assumptions regarding the course of history had been subjected to devastating criticism by Jacob Burckhardt[9] and Friedrich Nietzsche.[10] These pessimistic notes recurred in philosophic discussions and reflections on the state of modern culture throughout the first half of the twentieth century, but they did not seriously affect the thought of practicing historians until the 1960s. In many ways the 1960s were a turning point at which the consciousness of a crisis of modern society and culture, long in preparation, came to a head. Only then did the conditions created by World War II become obvious, among them the end of the colonial empires and a greater awareness that non-Western peoples also had a history.[11] Within the Western societies the older conceptions of a national consensus, reiterated in writings of the 1950s,[12] was replaced by a greater awareness of the diversities within the established nation states. Michael Harrington's *The Other America* (1961)[13] portrayed a very different picture of American society than the optimistic views held by historians such as Daniel Boorstin[14] and sociologists such as Daniel Bell.[15] But Marxist conceptions of class appeared inadequate in an environment that was increasingly aware of other divisions such as gender, race, ethnicity, and life style. The shift from an industrial to an information society further affected consciousness. For the first time there was an intense awareness of the negative sides of economic growth with its threat to a stable environment. The full impact of the Holocaust sank into public awareness, not immediately at the end of the World War II, but only at a distance when a new generation acquired a critical stance. The destructive qualities of the civilizing process increasingly moved into the center of awareness.

For the historian this transformation of consciousness had

several consequences. It marked for many the end of a "grand narrative."[16] The West increasingly appeared as merely one among a number of civilizations, none of which could claim primacy. Similarly modernity lost its unique quality. Oswald Spengler had relatively early spoken of a plurality of civilizations each of which for him, however, followed a developmental pattern.[17] Marc Bloch and Fernand Braudel already in the 1930s and 1940s turned from a narrative history that followed a sequence of events to one that examined conditions in a specific time period.[18] From a very different perspective, Burckhardt had already attempted something similar.[19] And even a specific epoch did not constitute an integrated unit, as Braudel stressed when he examined the sixteenth century from three different time perspectives.[20] Time in the Newtonian sense as an objective entity or in the Kantian sense of a universal category of thought no longer existed. Historical time varied for Braudel with the subject of its study, each with a different speed and rhythm, whether the historian dealt with the great overarching structures within which natural or social, economic, and cultural history underwent gradual changes, or with the rapid pulse of political history. Moreover, even within a set social framework, differing conceptions of time coexisted or competed, as in Jacques Le Goff's distinction between the time of the clergy and of the merchant in the Middle Ages,[21] or Edward P. Thompson's view of the confrontation of preindustrial and industrial time in an age of emergent industrial capitalism.[22] The claims of segments of the population previously excluded from historical narratives, foremost among them women and ethnic minorities, led to the creation of new histories sometimes integrated into a larger narrative, but often apart from it.

This fragmentation of the subject matter of history did not in itself constitute a repudiation of historical interest. In many ways the scope of historical writing has expanded enormously in the past thirty years. The newer histories indeed challenged the traditional historiography, which had concentrated on political and social elites, and demanded the inclusion of those segments of the population that had long been neglected. They offered "a history from below," which not only included women but also introduced a feminist perspective. They also challenged the social science approaches, which had placed great impersonal structures at the center of history and in doing so had no more questioned the existing power relationships than had the older political history. If the social science-oriented history had sought to replace the study of politics with that of society, the new history turned to the study of culture understood as the conditions of everyday life and everyday experience. From this perspective, the Marxist emphasis on the central role of politics and economics as the locus of power and exploitation remained too impervious to the real interests and concerns of live human beings. Rather than a decline in historical interest, the past three decades have seen a veritable explosion in historical writings as various segments of the population have sought to establish their identities apart from the larger, traditional, national wholes.

The questioning of the possibility of conducting objective historical inquiry at all constituted a more serious challenge. Increasingly, disillusionment with the quality of modern Western civilization brought about a profound reaction against the modern scientific outlook. Anthropologists such as Claude Lévi-Strauss denied that modern scientific rationality offered any advantage over "savage" mythical thought in seeking to come to terms with life.[23] From Ranke's systematization of source criticism in the 1820s to Robert Fogel's attempts in the 1970s to transform history into a science working with quantifiable theoretical models,[24] historians assumed that there are objects of historical research accessible to clearly defined methods of inquiry. This confidence corresponded to the strict dividing line between historical and literary discourse and to the separation between the way a historian who viewed himself as a scientist worked and that of the popular writer of history more aware of the literary qualities of his work. Nietzsche had already in his early writings, *The Birth of Tragedy* (1872) and *Of the Usefulness and Disadvantage of History for Life)* (1874), denied the possibility as well as the utility of historical research and scholarly historiography. He believed not only that the object of research was determined by the interests and biases of the historian but that the conviction on which occidental thinking since Socrates and Plato had been based, namely that there is an objective truth not tied to the subjectivity of the thinker, was untenable.

For Nietzsche, as for Marx before him, knowledge was a means of exerting power.[25] But Nietzsche did not share Marx's confidence that the unmasking of the ideological factors that entered into knowledge could lead to objective knowledge. The history of philosophical reason since Socrates seemed to him to be a form of unreason, an effective means of asserting authority and power. Thus he denied the priority of logical, for example Socratic, over prelogical, that is mythical or poetic, thinking.

From this point of departure an increasing number of historians in recent decades arrived at the conviction that history is connected more closely to literature than to science. This notion has challenged the very assumptions on which modern historical scholarship has rested. The idea that objectivity in historical research is not possible because there is no object of history has gained increasing currency. Accordingly the historian is always the prisoner of the world within which he thinks, and his thoughts and perceptions are conditioned by the categories of the language in which he operates. Thus language shapes reality but does not refer to it.[26] This idea arose particularly in linguistic and literary theory since the 1960s,[27] although the basic conception of language with which it worked had been foreshadowed in Ferdinand de Saussure's *Course in General Linguistics* published in 1916,[28] which saw language as a self-contained system. Roland Barthes in the 1960s[29] and Hayden White in the 1970s[30] stressed the literary character of historical texts and the fictional elements they inevitably contained. Developing further de Saussure's conception of language as a self-contained system of signs, literary theorists in France and the United States, such as Jacques Derrida and Paul de Man, argued that language constructs reality rather than referring to it. The historian works with texts, but these texts do not refer to an outside world. In Derrida's well-known aphorism, "there is nothing outside of the text."[31] The text does not have to have a written or verbal form. Cultures, as anthropologists such as Clifford Geertz would maintain, are also texts.[32] But not only are texts nonreferential, they also have no unambiguous meaning. Every text can be read in innumerable ways. The author's intention no longer matters, not only because it is multilayered and contradictory, but also because the text exists independently of the author. Applied to history this means that in the final analysis every historical work is a literary work which has to be judged by categories of literary criticism.

This is a line of argumentation that has been steadily pursued in French and American literary theory since Barthes's formulation of it in the 1960s. Barthes denied the distinction between history and literature and with it that between fact and fiction which has generally been accepted in Western thought since Aristotle formulated it in his *Poetics*. This critique of historical realism has been linked to a critique of modern society and culture. Thus Barthes complained that "the realism of historical discourse is part of a general cultural pattern . . . [that] points to an alienating fetishism of the 'real,' by which men seek to escape from their freedom and their role as makers of meaning."[33] In a similar vein Hayden White noted "the reluctance to consider historical narratives as what they most manifestly are: verbal fictions, the contents of which are more *invented* than *found* and the forms of which have more in common with their counterparts in literature than they have with those in the sciences."[34] Carrying the critique of the supposed authority in modern society even further, Hans Kellner charged that "'truth' and 'reality' are, of course, the primary authoritarian weapons of our time."[35] What this amounts to is the negation of the way in which historians have done historical research since Classical antiquity and more specifically since the professionalization of historical studies. As Robert Berkhofer noted: "Because normal historians try to reconcile variant interpretations by *reference* to facts rather than by arguments over the nature of narratives as such, they must presume in practice that factuality possesses some sort of coercive reality." Since it denies factuality, "contemporary literary theory defies the very intellectual foundation of current historical practice."[36]

Yet the critics of historical realism who insisted on the autonomy of texts seldom went beyond theoretical statements to confront a concrete historical subject matter, which for them could only be a linguistic construct. The proponents of the movement that defined itself as "New Historicism"[37] dealt more directly with literature and culture in a historical context, specifically that of Elizabethan England[38] approached through its literary productions, and also the European encounter with the original inhabitants of the New World.[39] These two groups shared basic assumptions of postmodernist literary theory regarding the centrality of language and its opaqueness, as well as anthropological conceptions of cultures as symbolic networks of meaning. Nevertheless the New Historicists rejected the notion of the autonomy of texts and rather saw texts as part of complex symbolic negotiations that reflected power relations understood partly in Foucaultian but partly also in Marxist terms. The texts that formed the bases of their analyses were informed by the same cultural dialectics as society at large in which since the early modern period capitalist market forces had operated. For them, as for the sociologist Pierre Bourdieu, these forces assumed the form not of material but of culturally negotiable symbolic capital. Stressing the multiple meanings of all literary and cultural texts, they remained as critical of the practices of "normal history" as did the practitioners of postmodernist literary theory. They aimed for what Stephen Greenblatt, the initiator of New Historicism, called a "Poetics of Culture."[40]

The radical critiques of accepted methods of historical inquiry that have dominated theoretical discussions of history from the 1970s to the present have had an important but nevertheless limited impact on the writing of history. Were one to accept the premises of this critique, meaningful historical writing would be impossible. Clearly history has literary qualities. The historian, as F. A. Ankersmit has argued,[41] always uses metaphors to create historical images. The difference between what he calls the modern historiography of both the Rankean and the social science orientation and the postmodern position lies in the latter's insistence on the metaphorical, nonreferential character of every historical text and the former's illusory conviction that there is a historical substance separate from the historian's prose or poetry. Hans Kellner, in a similar vein, has seen the whole tradition of modern historical scholarship as an aberration from the older, premodern conception of history as a form of rhetoric.[42]

But the matter is obviously not that simple. For even the historians prior to the period of professionalization viewed themselves as rhetoricians for whom history was to contain exemplars, lessons for life, and were at the same time committed to telling a truthful story. The tenor of recent discussions, such as the panel on "Fictionality, Narrativity, Objectivity" at the International Congress of Historical Sciences in Montreal in 1995,[43] was to occupy a middle position, to recognize, as Roger Chartier formulated it, that while "one among many forms of narration, history is nevertheless singular in that it maintains a special relationship to truth. More precisely its narrative constructions aim at reconstructing a past that really was. This reference to a reality pre-existing the historical text and situated outside it, of which the text has the function of producing an intelligible account . . . is what constitutes history and keeps it different from fable or falsification."[44]

This distinction between truth and falsehood remains fundamental to the work of the historian. The concept of truth has become immeasurably more complex in the course of recent critical thought. To be sure the postulate of "an absolute objectivity and scientificity of historical knowledge is no longer accepted without reservation."[45] Nevertheless the concept of truth and with it the duty of the historian to avoid and to uncover falsification has by no means been abandoned. As a trained professional he continues to work critically with the sources that make access to the past reality possible. The distinction between rationality and irrationality in historical investigation rests not on an abstract concept of truth or objectivity but on "the idea of history as an interpretive community, a practicing discipline with professional standards."[46]

The flight from the reality of the past in recent literary, linguistic, and historical thought reflects a deep discontent with the alienating aspects of modern civilization. Insofar as science occupied a central role in this civilization, scientific approaches, including the modern tradition of scholarly history, came under attack. This critique, of course, also had political implications. What had begun in the nineteenth century and in the first half of the twentieth century with Burckhardt, Nietzsche, and later Heidegger as a rejection of the humanistic heritage of the Enlightenment from an elitist, antidemocratic perspective was taken up after 1945 by thinkers such as Jean-Paul Sartre and the Frankfurt School—Theodor Adorno and Max Horkheimer— who occupied positions generally more closely identified with the left, but who no longer saw in the Enlightenment faith in reason and science a means of liberating human beings but, on the contrary, a means of controlling and manipulating them.[47] If the Enlightenment had sought to free men from myths and illusions, its critics sought to free human beings from the ethical meaninglessness that in their opinion the rational—or in their view rationalistic—approach to life and reality implied. Scientific reason suddenly became a monster. Foucault and Derrida agreed that, by putting abstract reason in the center, the Western tradition of philosophy since Socrates had legitimized patterns of domination[48] and, for Joan Scott writing from a feminist perspective, had established patriarchal authority in the very language of common discourse.[49]

This postmodern critique contained important valid points. It demonstrated that the notion of a unitary history was not tenable, that history was marked not only by continuity but also by ruptures. The critics rightly point to the ideological assumptions that have been embedded in the dominant discourse of professional historical scholarship. They also rightly challenge its exaggerated claims of speaking with the authority of experts. Nevertheless, they tend to throw out the baby with the bathwater when they deny the possibility of any kind of rational historical discourse and question the notion of historical truth and with it that of historical falsity. They thus eliminate not only the admittedly fluid border that lies between historical discourse, which always involves fictional elements, and fiction, which mostly seeks to interpret reality, but also that which lies between honest scholarship and propaganda. This blurring of borders has become particularly troublesome in recent discussions on the Holocaust as a historical event.[50] The contradictions of resolving history into purely imaginative literature become apparent in Hayden White's admission that from a moral perspective it is unacceptable to deny the reality of the Holocaust, yet it is impossible in a historical narrative to establish objectively that it happened.[51]

The postmodernist challenge has had a significant impact on historical thought and writing without, however, destroying the continuities with older conceptions and practices. Postmodernism reflects a society and culture in transformation in which old certainties regarding industrial growth, rising economic expectations, and traditional middle-class norms have been shaken. This has been reflected in the historiography of the past twenty years. The subject matter of history has shifted from social structures and processes to culture in the broad sense of everyday life. History has again assumed a human face as new attention has been given to individuals, this time not to the high and mighty but to common folks. A school of historians has sought to replace the study of macrohistorical and macrosocial processes by what they have termed microhistory, concentrating on small social units consisting of concrete individuals. The new emphasis on the culture of everyday life brought history into close contact with the anthropology of Clifford Geertz. "Believing, with Max Weber, that man is an animal suspended in webs of significance he himself has spun," Geertz "take[s] culture to be those webs and the analysis of it therefore not an experimental science in search of law but an interpretive one in search of meaning. It is explication . . . construing social expressions [that] on their surface [are] enigmatical" that the student of culture is after. Thus the new cultural history, like the "hermeneutics" of classical historicism, is concerned not with explanation but with "explication," the attempt to reconstruct the significance of the social expressions that serve as its texts.[52]

Yet the hermeneutics of the new history differed from that of the Rankean school. The latter not only dealt with a different subject matter, that of leading personalities within the framework of great political institutions, but also assumed that the texts contained a clear meaning that could be reconstructed through philological analysis. Ranke and his school still believed that history was a strict science, even if different in subject matter and methods from that of the explanatory sciences. For the new cultural history, the central institutions of state, church, and the world market had crumbled, and the meaning of the texts was no longer transparent but was marked by contradictions and ruptures.

All this lent support to the postmodernist attacks against notions of objectivity and scientific method, which ended by abolishing the distinction between historical and fictional narrative. Yet an examination of the historiography of the past twenty years, which I undertake in this volume, suggests rather that, while historians became much more guarded in their belief in the authority of science, they nevertheless worked with the conviction that the historian dealt with a real and not an imagined past and that this real past, although accessible only through the medium of the historian's mind, nevertheless called for methods and approaches that followed a logic of inquiry. It is striking that while postmodern thought increasingly called into question the authority of the professional scholar, historical work in fact felt the pressures of increasing professionalization. Although there were calls in the late twentieth century, by the History Workshop movement,[53] for interested citizens outside the universities to dig for their roots, in fact the new cultural history was carried out almost entirely at the universities. A good deal of the challenge to the scientific ethos in historical work came from outside the disciplines—from literary theorists and critics who wished to collapse history into imaginative literature. Yet strikingly, literary criticism itself, once the domain of independent intellectuals writing in journals and reviews, increasingly was imprisoned in the confines of academe. Notwithstanding basic philosophical reorientations, the culture of academe, including its criteria for acquiring the credentials necessary to obtain a position and have a successful career, has remained remarkably constant from the launching of professional historiography at the German universities in the early nineteenth century to the present. Thus despite the calls for the repudiation of a scientific ethos the scientific ethos persisted in practice.

This was essential if there was to be meaningful historical work. History continued to be a learned craft. The historians of the 1970s and 1980s learned from the anthropologists the significance of culture in the understanding of political and social behavior. Thus studies of the French Revolution took on a new direction. The stress on class and economic factors that had informed the Marxist analyses of Georges Lefebvre[54] and Albert Soboul[55] and the anti-Marxist analysis of Alfred Cobban[56] in the mid-twentieth century was replaced by a stronger emphasis on culture, language, symbols, and rituals in the writings of François Furet,[57] Lynn Hunt,[58] William Sewell,[59] and Simon Schama[60] in the 1980s and early 1990s. But ultimately the new cultural historians, like their traditional forebears, had to go to the archives, too. Although they were highly critical of the assumptions of the earlier social sciences approaches, they nevertheless, often with the aid of modern computer techniques, utilized empirical findings to create a foundation for their interpretative reconstruction of local culture.

While the work of the 1970s and 1980s frequently emphasized the significance of culture at the expense of politics and of broader social processes, the events since 1989 have made it clear that the latter cannot be ignored. While it is difficult after the enormities of our century to follow modernization theory in endowing the civilization of the West with any special dignity or to view history as a unitary process, it is nevertheless clear that the powerful forces described by that theory are indeed operative in the modern world. To be sure, modernization theory has generally been overly optimistic in viewing the modern world as the "end of history,"[61] the outcome of a benign process. Moreover, the collapse of the Soviet empire has shown the inadequacy of an exclusive reliance on political, economic, or cultural analysis, while the persistence of older nationalistic and religious attitudes and their transformation under modern conditions, as manifested in the ethnic conflicts and outbursts of religious fundamentalism of recent years, have further exposed the limits of modernization theory. What is needed in its stead is a broad historical approach that takes both cultural and institutional aspects into consideration. The postmodern critique of traditional science and traditional historiography has offered important correctives to historical thought and practice. It has not destroyed the historian's commitment to recapturing reality or his or her belief in a logic of inquiry, but it has demonstrated the complexity of both. Perhaps we can see in the history of historiography an ongoing dialogue that, while it never reaches finality, contributes to a broadening of perspective.

. . .

Our story begins with the professionalization of historical studies in the nineteenth century. Historiography is, of course, much older. Human beings have dealt with their past in all cultures, but the ways in which they have done so have differed. Thus in the Western, including the Islamic, world, but also in East Asia, written history has occupied an important role, but so have nonwritten forms of history, monuments, symbols, and popular traditions. At least as early as Herodotus and Thucydides in the West and Ssu'ma Chi'en in the East a conscious effort was made to distinguish history from myth and to arrive at a truthful description of past events. Nevertheless there was no attempt to claim for history the status of a science similar in its rigor to the natural sciences. The pursuit of history as a literary genre seeking to recapture past reality truthfully and honestly but in an aesthetically elegant manner persisted from Classical Western and East Asian antiquity until relatively recently. Only in the nineteenth century was history transformed into a professionalized discipline that viewed itself as a "science" practiced by professionally trained historians.

English speakers are not comfortable with the term "historical science" (*Geschichtswissenschaft*), commonly used in continental European but also East Asian languages to distinguish history as a discipline from history as a literary pursuit. The term is not common in the English language, where science generally denotes the systematic natural sciences or a logic of inquiry and explanation modeled on the natural sciences, as in the systematic approach and proclivity to abstraction to be found in the "social sciences." In the languages of the continent, *Wissenschaft* (German), *science* (French), *scienza* (Italian), *ciencia* (Spanish), or *nauk* (Russian) denote a systematic approach to any sphere of knowledge, including the humanities, guided by methods of investigation accepted by a community of scholars.

We shall use the term in this book to refer to the modern discipline of history. The emergence of historical science in this sense coincided with the establishment of history as a professional discipline taught and studied at the universities. The discipline has never had the conceptual rigor of the natural sciences or of the analytical social sciences because of the elements of volition, intention, and meaning in human behavior that defy the degree of abstraction in which knowledge resides in the harder sciences. Nevertheless it demands adherence to a logic of scholarly inquiry shared by scholars generally by which the results of historical inquiry can be tested for their validity very much as they are in other disciplines. It also expects the scholar to go beyond the raw data yielded by his sources to create a coherent account that, like all scientific discourse, involves explanation. The nature of explanation obviously differs in historiography from that in the hard sciences because it has to take into account not only the intention and individuality of its objects of study but the role of the researcher's subjectivity as well, clearly greater in historical studies than in the hard sciences. Thomas Kuhn has argued that, even in physics, conceptions of what constitutes scientific work are not exclusively the result of developments and discussions internal to the discipline but are closely tied to the broader intellectual currents of the culture within which scientific work takes place.[62] If this applies to a discipline like physics, which emphatically seeks to exclude elements of subjectivity in scientific judgment, it applies even more to history, which recognizes the role of subjectivity as an inescapable element in scholarly investigation.

The above is not meant to suggest that the work of the scientist or of the historian can be explained primarily in terms of social factors or that it has primarily an ideological function. But it means that science, and especially "historical science," which is so closely tied to human values and intentions, must be seen in the sociocultural and political framework in which it is practiced. A history of historiography that takes into consideration only factors internal to the discipline of history is not possible. It is conceivable that a set of historical facts can be examined by means of critical standards on which there is a consensus in the discipline; the same consensus can hardly be attained when these facts are set into a broader context of events and development. As I have indicated, science, and this includes historical science, can never be reduced to a set of disembodied processes of thought internal to the discipline, but always involves living human beings who work within the framework of scholarly and scientific institutions and hold assumptions regarding the nature of reality that they share with a great many of their contemporaries. Science always presupposes a community of scholars who share practices of research and forms of communication. It is therefore not possible to separate a history of historiography from the institutions and the social and intellectual setting in which scholarly work takes place.

The three parts of this book will deal with the establishment of history as a scholarly discipline, the challenge of the social sciences to the traditional scholarship, and finally the critique of social science approaches by postmodernist thought and its effect on the work of the historian.

I

The Early Phase: The Emergence of History as a Professional Discipline

Chapter 1

Classical Historicism as a Model for Historical Scholarship

In the early nineteenth century a radical change took place in the Western world generally in the way history was researched, written, and taught as it was transformed into a professional discipline. Until then there had been two dominant traditions of writing history: one predominantly learned and antiquarian, the other essentially literary. Only occasionally, as in the work of the great British historians of the eighteenth century, Gibbon, Hume, and Robertson, did these two traditions coalesce. The new discipline of history that emerged at the German universities stressed the learned side of history, yet at the same time it freed learning from narrow antiquarianism, and its best practitioners maintained a sense for literary quality. It is important to keep in mind that the new historical profession served definite public needs and political aims that made it important to communicate the results of its research to a public whose historical consciousness it sought to shape and who turned to the historians in search of their own historical identity. Thus there existed from the beginning a tension between the scientific ethos of the profession, which demanded a commitment free of preconceptions and value judgments, and the political function of the profession, which took a certain social order for granted.

This tension was reflected in the educational mission the nineteenth-century university set for itself. The prototype of this university was the University of Berlin, founded in 1810 as part of the reorganization of secondary and higher education carried out by Wilhelm von Humboldt in Prussia in the reform era following Prussia's disastrous defeat by Napoleon in 1806 and 1807. These reforms, sometimes described as a "revolution from above," laid the basis for modern economic, legal, and social conditions, similar to those the French Revolution had effected but within a political framework that maintained a great deal of its old monarchical, bureaucratic, military, and aristocratic structure. The civil service, recruited heavily from the university-educated middle class, played a central role in a political order in which representative institutions functioned as yet only on the communal level. Humboldt sought to reform the *Gymnasia* and the university with the aim of providing a comprehensive intellectual and aesthetic education, the core of what came to be known as *Bildung*,[1] by means of which the foundation was to be laid for a society of informed and dedicated citizens. The reforms were by no means intended to be democratic. The humanistic education, with its heavy reliance on the Latin and especially the Greek classics, not only deepened the gulf between an educated *Bürgertum* and the general population but also created a class of higher public servants whom Fritz Ringer has compared with the Chinese mandarins.[2]

The new university embodied this fusion of *Wissenschaft* and *Bildung*. In contrast to the universities of the old regime, whose prime function was instruction, the University of Berlin was to become a center in which teaching was informed by research. With this in mind, Leopold Ranke was called to the University of Berlin in 1825. Ranke, a young teacher at the *Gymnasium* in Frankfurt/Oder, had just published a book in which he sought to reconstruct, on the basis of a critical examination of documents, a great transformation in European politics: the emergence as a prime factor in international politics of the modern state systems and the balancing of the great powers that took place in the course of the Italian wars of the late fifteenth and early sixteenth centuries.[3] In a methodological appendix[4] to the book, he rejected any attempt to write history on the basis of other than primary sources, accusing somewhat injustly all previous accounts of the Italian wars, including the classical works of Guicciardini, of failing totally to examine the evidence critically. It was Ranke's aim to turn history into a rigorous science practiced by professionally trained historians. Like Thucydides, who was the subject of his dissertation, he sought to write a history that combined a trustworthy reconstruction of the past with literary elegance. History needed to be written *by* specialists, but not only or even primarily *for* them, but for a broad educated public. History was to be both a scientific discipline and a source of culture.

Ranke's conception of history as a rigorous science is characterized by the tension between the explicit demand for objective research, which strictly rejects all value judgments and metaphysical speculations, and the implicit philosophic and political assumptions that actually determine his research. For Ranke, scholarly research was intimately connected with critical method. A thorough training in the methods of philological criticism was a necessary precondition. Ranke introduced seminars in which future historians were trained in the critical examination of medieval documents. The seminar itself was not entirely new. Johann Christoph Gatterer had introduced something similar at the University of Göttingen in the 1770s, but only Ranke made it an integral component of the training of historians. By 1848 all German-speaking universities had adopted it. Ranke's understanding of rigorous scholarship presupposed strict abstinence from value judgments. As he stated in the famous introductory passage in his initial book on the Italian wars, which won him the call to Berlin, the historian was to refrain from "judging the past" and limit himself to "showing how things actually happened."[5] Yet at the same time he rejected any sort of positivism that would view the establishment of facts as the essential task of the historian's work. Whereas for Max Weber at the turn of the twentieth century a rigorous historical approach revealed the ethical meaninglessness of existence, for Ranke it reflected a world of meaning and of values. Thus he wrote: "While the philosopher, viewing history from his vantage point, seeks infinity merely in progression, development, and totality, history recognizes something infinite in every existence: in every condition, in every being, something eternal, coming from God."[6] History thus replaced philosophy as the science that provided insights into the meaning of the human world.

Far from showing the relativity and hence meaninglessness of all values, the "impartial" (*unpartheyisch*)[7] way of looking at things for which Ranke argued in fact revealed the ethical character of social institutions as they had developed historically. Although replacing Hegel's philosophic approach by a historical one, Ranke agreed with Hegel that the existing political states, insofar as they were the results of historical growth, constituted "moral energies,"[8] "thoughts of God."[9] Ranke thus arrived at a position close to that of Edmund Burke, arguing that any challenge to the established political and social institutions by revolutionary means or extensive reforms constituted a violation of the historical spirit.[10] The "impartial" approach to the past, seeking merely to show "what had actually happened," thus in fact for Ranke revealed the existing order as God had willed it. For Ranke, very much as for Hegel, the history of the modern world revealed the solidity of the political and social institutions of Restoration Prussia, in which civic liberty and private property existed and prospered under the aegis of a strong monarchy and an enlightened civil service. Hence the centrality of the state in Ranke's conception of history. One cannot understand the new science of history as it was understood by Ranke without taking into account the political and religious context in which it emerged. What at first appeared to be a paradox, the professionalization of scholarship with its demand of strict objectivity on the one hand and the political and cultural role of the historian on the other, thus turns out not to be a paradox at all.

Ranke ultimately became the model for professionalized historical scholarship in the nineteenth century. Before 1848, however, he was not at all typical of German, and even less so of international, historiography. The Enlightenment tradition of cultural history was still very much alive in the writings of Heeren, Schlosser, Gervinus, and others who much more openly espoused political causes and were aware of the need for critical philological methods but declined to make them a fetish. The intense historical interest in Europe resulted in the launching of large-scale undertakings to edit and publish the sources of national history. Already in the eighteenth century Muratori launched such an enterprise in Italy, the *Rerum italicarum scrip-*

tores. In Germany the *Monumenta Germaniae Historica* were begun in the 1820s as a vast collection of sources of German medieval history. The *Collection de documents inédits sur l'histoire de France* and the *Chronicles and Memorials of Great Britain and Ireland During the Middle Ages* undertook something similar for France and the British Isles. In 1821 the Ecole des Chartes was founded in Paris to train historians and archivists in the critical examination of sources. While this suggested a relatively narrow learnedness, the mainstream of historical writing in France, Great Britain, and the United States, as the names of Jules Michelet, Thomas Babington Macaulay, and George Bancroft suggest, wrote for a broad public.

Measured by the role of historians in public life, history was perhaps valued even more highly in France than in Germany. Thus François Guizot, Jules Michelet, Louis Blanc, Alphonse de Lamartine, Alexis de Tocqueville, Hippolyte Taine, and Adolphe Thiers all occupied positions in French politics not equaled in Germany. Perhaps this was so because historical studies in France were less professionalized and thereby less cut off from the general educated public than in Germany, where the historians were increasingly located at the universities with and subjected to specific scholarly demands. The different political culture in Germany and France may partly explain the openness of French historians such as Guizot, Thierry, Blanc, and Tocqueville to social issues, in contrast to the much greater focus on political and diplomatic history in Germany.

After 1848 in Germany, and after 1870 in most European countries, the United States, and Japan—somewhat later in Great Britain and the Netherlands—historical studies underwent professionalization. The German model was generally followed: in the United States in the introduction of the Ph.D. program at Johns Hopkins University in 1872, in France already in 1868 with the foundation of the Ecole Pratique des Hautes Etudes in Paris with its focus on research. The seminar began to replace or at least to supplement the lecture. Journals were founded that propagated the new methods of scientific scholarship. Thus the founding of the *Historische Zeitschrift* (1859) was followed by the *Revue Historique* (1876), the *Rivista Storica Italiana* (1884), the *English Historical Review* (1886), the *Ameri-*

can Historical Review (1895), and similar journals in other countries. Significantly the first issue of the *English Historical Review* opened with an article by Lord Acton on "German Schools of History."[11] The American Historical Association, founded in 1884, chose Ranke, "the father of historical science,"[12] as its first honorary member. Generally the shift to the German model meant a retreat from a broader cultural history to one more narrowly focused on politics. The tension we observed in Ranke between the demand that strict scholarship should avoid value judgments and the actual commitment of historiography to political and social values also occurred in the new professional history. In fact the tremendous increase in historical scholarship in the nineteenth century was closely related to the political and social setting. Not only in Germany but also in France, historical studies took place at universities and institutes sponsored by the state. And despite the academic freedom the professoriat enjoyed, the recruitment process, in which the state played a role, guaranteed a high degree of conformity.[13]

The dominant consensus was admittedly different in Germany and in France, reflecting different political cultures, but both were deeply rooted in the values of the firmly established middle classes, *Bürgertum* or bourgeoisie. In both countries historiography consciously espoused liberal positions that differed from Ranke's conservatism. In France this liberalism identified itself especially after 1871 with the republican tradition. It was laic and anticlerical and confronted the Catholicism of the royalists.[14] In Germany after the defeat of the 1848 Revolution it sought the fulfillment of liberal social and economic aims within the semiautocratic Hohenzollern monarchy. Thus a very different myth of the national past emerged in the histories of Michelet or Lavisse in France or those of Sybel and Treitschke in Germany. What is striking is how professionalization, with the development of the scientific ethos and scientific practices that accompanied it, led everywhere to an increasing ideologization of historical writing. Historians went into the archives to find evidence that would support their nationalistic and class preconceptions and thus give them the aura of scientific authority.

In general the new historical outlook, later often referred to by the term *historicism* (*Historismus*),[15] was hailed as an intellectual advance. Historicism was more than a theory of history. It involved a total philosophy of life, a unique combination of a conception of science, specifically of the human or cultural sciences, and a conception of the political and social order. It assumed, as Ortega y Gasset formulated it, that "Man, in a word, has no nature; what he has is . . . history."[16] But it also firmly believed that history revealed meaning and that meaning revealed itself only in history. Seen in this way, history became the only way of studying human affairs. Historians and social philosophers such as Ernst Troeltsch and Friedrich Meinecke then used the term *historicism* to identify the worldview dominant in the German academic world of the nineteenth century but also in the world of the solid *Bürgertum*. Friedrich Meinecke in 1936 spoke of historicism as "the highest point in the understanding of things human."[17] In theory this approach was to open up all spheres of human activity to historical study.

In fact it both widened and restricted the historical perspective. It is important to keep in mind that German historical scholarship assumed its modern form in the first two thirds of the nineteenth century, prior to the industrialization or democratization of German society, and that it bore the stamp of its time. Its basic assumptions remained largely unchanged after 1870, probably for three reasons: the tremendous prestige that German historical scholarship had attained by then, the particular political conditions in Germany after the failed revolution of 1848–49, and the subsequent course that unification took under Bismarck, which prevented the emergence of a democratic ethos in Germany. As we have seen, however, the German pattern of historical science became the model for professional studies elsewhere, under political and intellectual conditions different from those of Germany. Thus historians outside Germany adopted important elements of German scholarly practice without entirely understanding or wanting to understand the basic philosophic and political convictions connected with them. For instance, Ranke was often misunderstood as a positivist "determined to hold strictly to the facts, to preach no sermon, to point no moral, to adorn no tale, but to tell the simple historic truth."[18]

The theory of historicism held to Ranke's view that "every epoch is immediate to God."[19] In fact, however, not all epochs were regarded even by Ranke, who still had a broad European perspective, as of equal interest to the historian. Ranke wished to write world history, but world history for him was synonymous with the history of the Germanic and Latin peoples, of Central and Western Europe. "India and China," he wrote, "have a lengthy chronology" but at best have a "natural history,"[20] not history in the sense in which he understood it. After Ranke, the focus of historians narrowed further to restrict itself increasingly to the nations and to the political life of the nations. Historians felt compelled to go into the archives, which contained not only official documents of state but also much information of an administrative, economic, and social nature, which they mostly ignored. And while there had been occasional women historians prior to the nineteenth century, they now were almost totally absent from a profession that had no place for them.

By the turn of the century Ernst Troeltsch spoke of a "crisis of historicism."[21] He gave voice to the opinion, gaining in currency, that historical studies had demonstrated the relativity of all values and revealed the meaninglessness of existence. The "crisis of historicism,"[22] increasingly popular as a topic in German discussions after World War I, was thus seen as primarily a result of intellectual developments. This "crisis" was felt most keenly in Germany because there the early and mid-nineteenth-century philosophic assumptions were most out of step with the realities of the twentieth century. At risk was not only historicism, as a worldview rooted in the Idealism of German classical culture, but the entire culture of the German *Bürgertum* and its ideal of *Bildung*. Increasingly, historical scholarship, so central to the formation of national and social identity in the nineteenth century, had lost its relevance in public life. The progressive institutionalization of teaching and research and the pressure for specialization that accompanied it thus gradually dissolved the close relationship of *Wissenschaft* and *Bildung* that had characterized the great political historiography of the nineteenth century.

Chapter 2

The Crisis of Classical Historicism

Historical studies at the end of the nineteenth century were characterized by a sense of profound unease. Almost simultaneously throughout Europe and in the United States a critical examination of the presuppositions upon which the established historiography at the universities rested took place. No single concept emerged of how historical studies should be conducted in the modern age, but there was widespread conviction that the subject matter of history must be expanded and greater space be given to the role of society, the economy, and culture. Moreover the preference for a narrative, preeminently political, history centered on events and great personalities was challenged, and the demand was made that history be linked more closely to the empirical social sciences. At no point, however, did this critical reaction to history as it was researched and taught at universities throughout the world question two basic assumptions of the older historiography, namely (1) that history should be a professional discipline, and (2) that history must conceive of itself as a science. On the contrary, there was pressure to make the pursuit of history even more professional and more scientific.

In Germany this discussion gained in intensity with the controversy surrounding Karl Lamprecht's *Deutsche Geschichte* (German History), the first volume of which appeared in 1891.[1] Lamprecht questioned two basic principles of conventional historical scholarship: the central role assigned to the state and the concentration on persons and events. In the natural sciences, he asserted, the age in which scientific method restricted itself to the description of isolated phenomena has long been *passé*. Historical scholarship, too, would have to replace the descriptive method with a genetic one. Because of its broad scope, encompassing culture, society, and politics, and its readability, the *Deutsche Geschichte* was received very positively by a broad public. But it also met with vehement opposition from most professional historians. Their criticism was justified on two grounds: First, the work contained many mistakes and imprecisions, giving rise to the assumption that it had been hastily and carelessly composed, but not necessarily invalidating its basic theses. Second, the latter were open to criticism because they employed a highly speculative conception of collective psychology to prove that German history since antiquity had followed predetermined laws of historical development. The concept of law was also central to Lamprecht's understanding of science. In his programmatic writings he distinguished between the "old directions in historical science"—the endeavor to establish facts by means of rigorous research in the sources but without any "scientific" method for explaining historical behavior—and the "new" ones—the conscious approach to a subject of research by means of theoretical questions and methodological principles, as is done in every other science.[2] According to Lamprecht the older concept of scientific or scholarly inquiry into history rested on the metaphysical assumption that, behind the appearances observed by the historian, great historical forces or "ideas" were at work, giving history its coherence. The "new historical science" aimed at aligning history with the systematic social sciences; yet Lamprecht's key concept in the *Deutsche Geschichte*, that of a *Volksseele*, a national spirit that remained constant through all ages, had its roots in German romantic philosophy rather than in serious social science. This led Max Weber, who clearly advocated social science approaches in historical studies, to view Lamprecht's *Deutsche Geschichte* as speculative nonsense and to accuse Lamprecht of having "compromised for decades" a "good thing, namely the effort to steer historical work in the direction of greater conceptualization."[3]

Political motives also played an important role in the opposition to Lamprecht. For the key spokesmen of the profession, historical studies, as they had developed at the German universities in the nineteenth century, and the conception of history and science on which they rested, were closely linked to the political order that had resulted from German unification under Bismarck's leadership.[4] Already several years before the Lamprecht controversy erupted, there had been a sharp dispute between Dietrich Schäfer,[5] who represented the dominant views in the profession, and Eberhard Gothein,[6] who argued for the extension of history to include economic, social, and cultural aspects. For Schäfer the state was central to history; the German state as created by Bismarck was for him the prototype of the modern state. Unless one placed the state at the center of events, no coherent historical account was possible. But because he saw the state as an accumulation of power and therefore viewed foreign policy as the determining element of politics, Schäfer rejected any attempt to analyze politics from the perspective of domestic social forces or interests. Lamprecht was certainly anything but a revolutionary. He was definitely not opposed to the existing monarchical order nor to the global aims of the German *Reich*. Like many of his contemporaries, he rather wanted to strengthen and modernize Germany as a world power by integrating the alienated workers into the nation. Nevertheless his *Deutsche Geschichte*, critics maintained, contained elements in close affinity with materialistic, in some ways even Marxist[7] conceptions, which questioned the central role of the state and therefore the political and social order of the German Reich.

The almost total rejection of Lamprecht and of cultural and social history generally doubtless had a good deal to do with the homogeneity of the German historical profession. The mechanisms of recruitment into it, involving a long and tedious second dissertation (*Habilitation*) that could be rejected by a single secret negative vote from the full professors, made it virtually impossible for political and ideological nonconformists to obtain university positions. The result was not only that Lamprecht remained isolated as a historian, but also that attempts at introducing social history were hampered for a long time.[8] It was in neighboring historical disciplines such as economics and later, in the 1920s, in sociology that important work was done in social history. Lamprecht's influence in the long run was greatest in local and regional history (*Landesgeschichte*), which were less directly related to national politics and thus more inclined to deal with social and cultural aspects.

In France and America historians proved more open to establishing a closer relationship between historiography and the social sciences. Undoubtedly the very different political setting in those countries had something to do with this. While in Germany social history was forced on the defensive, in France it was sociology that led the fight against the traditional historical research as practiced at the universities. Emile Durkheim in 1888, in his "Cours de science sociale,"[9] denied history the rank of a science, because it was concerned with the particular and therefore did not aim at general statements capable of empirical validation, which constituted the core of scientific procedure and thought. History could at best be an auxiliary science supplying information for sociology, which, unlike history, was capable of becoming a rigorous science. According to the economist François Simiand,[10] who was strongly influenced by Durkheim, economic history was a subdivision of history compatible with social science because it worked with quantities and models. This was not possible for the conventional forms of narrative history.

While in the campaign against Lamprecht in Germany the fear of democratization played an important role, in the United States the "New Historians," who also designated themselves as "Progressive Historians"[11] and identified themselves with the goals of the "progressive era" in early twentieth-century America, set out to write a history for a modern democratic society. At a special section on "historical science" at the world exposition in Saint Louis in 1904 historians from Europe, specifically Karl Lamprecht and J. H. Bury, joined Frederick Jackson Turner, James Harvey Robinson, and Woodrow Wilson to agree on the need for reform in historical studies in the direction of interdisciplinarity.[12]

Although new interest arose in social history and in the social sciences, no single paradigm emerged. As we shall see, the new concern with social history went in several directions, varying along national lines and reflecting different ideological outlooks.

Yet despite all differences, the new concerns shared several basic assumptions with the older scholarly orientations. As we have already mentioned, one important characteristic they had in common was their view of themselves as professional historians. The New Historians too were situated in academic institutions, in departments or institutes of history. This meant that they were expected by their institutions to have similar credentials and fulfill similar scholarly requirements as their more traditional, older colleagues. And no matter how differently they conceived of their historical work, they agreed that history was a scientific enterprise that proceeded according to rigorous methodological guidelines.

The New Historians continued to be just as committed as the older ones to the presupposition that the scholarly and scientific writing of history required a rigorous critical examination and evaluation of the sources. Historians continued to receive training in research techniques very similar to that received by the older historians. In many ways their conception of the historian's ethos remained unchanged, and they shared assumptions about the course of history. Like the older school, they were firmly convinced of the quality of modern Western civilization. They also saw history as a unitary process that, whether they affirmed explicit theories of progress or not, pointed upward. And despite their avowal of democratic values, New Historians such as Frederick Jackson Turner, in accord with the dominant mood of imperialism, shared the idea of the white man's burden and excluded Blacks from their conception of American democracy.

In the following four chapters we shall deal with four different directions of social science history in the twentieth century: the German tradition of economic and social history and later of historical sociology; forms of social science history, primarily in the United States; the French *Annales* school; and finally the reconstitution of social history in Germany after World War II. This choice is admittedly selective and represents only a small segment of the historical writing of the time. Nevertheless these orientations reflect important examples of historical thought in the twentieth century.

Chapter 3

Economic and Social History in Germany and the Beginnings of Historical Sociology

An early attempt to deal historically with the problems created by industrialization was made by the so-called "Younger Historical School of National Economy" in Germany, the most important representative of which was Gustav von Schmoller. This school stood firmly in the tradition of classical historicism in affirming that economics is not determined by strict, universally valid, mathematically formulable laws, as held by the classical English and Scottish political economy and by the Viennese economic theorist Menger, but that it can only be understood historically in the framework of the values and institutions of a people or nation (*Volk*). The Schmoller school shared two further assumptions of classical German historicism: the emphasis on the central role of the state and the insistence that historical study must keep close to archival sources. It identified itself with the Hohenzollern dynasty and the political order that Bismarck had created in the process of German unification, but it also argued for the possibility and necessity of reform, particularly in the integration of the workers into the German nation state. From this school came the first great empirical investigations about the living conditions of industrial workers as well as studies about the status and culture of artisans in the Middle Ages. Independently of this school, but sharing its basic methods and assumptions, Lamprecht in the 1880s wrote his economic history of the Moselle Valley in the late Middle Ages,[1] attempting a comprehensive reconstruction of the structures and mentalities of a region. Significantly Lamprecht in the subtitle of the work calls it a study of "material culture." For economic and social history this work based on careful examination of social, political, and economic sources was of greater and more lasting significance than his *Deutsche Geschichte*, which because of its controversial character and broad scope attracted greater attention at the time but represented much less solid scholarship.

Lacking in the empirical work of the Schmoller school was any in-depth consideration of the theoretical and methodological presuppositions on which their investigations rested. This unreflective way of working, which assumed that an historical account contains its own explanation, failed to satisfy a growing number of social historians. By the end of the century, several important Neo-Kantian philosophers, foremost among them Wilhelm Dilthey, Wilhelm Windelband, and Heinrich Rickert, had sought to work out a clearer methodology for what they called the human or cultural sciences (*Geisteswissenschaften*, *Kulturwissenschaften*), which they contrasted with the natural sciences.[2] Both methodologies required clear conceptualization if they wanted to claim the status of sciences. But while the aim of the latter was to arrive at "nomothetic" or generalizing formulations that "explained" in abstract terms the lawful, recurring pattern of a lifeless nature, the former applied "idiographic" (individualizing) methods as means to grasp and "understand" the meaning of human actions in concrete cultural, social, and historical settings. The question remained how the human or cultural sciences such as historical studies research could proceed from unique phenomena to broader social and historical contexts. Here Dilthey, Windelband, and Rickert provided no guidelines beyond Ranke's and Droysen's prescriptions earlier in the century: to immerse oneself in the subject matter of one's study, a process Ranke termed "*Einfühlung*" (empathy) and Dilthey described as "*Erlebnis*" (experience).

This intuitive approach, which constituted the heart of the historicist conception of science, was challenged by a number of very diverse thinkers who argued that even the human sciences needed more rigorous methods. Lamprecht, as we already saw, had contended that history must apply rigorous analytical categories, without, however, succeeding in doing so in his own work. Already in 1884, the Viennese economist Carl Menger in his polemical work *Die Irrtümer des Historismus in der deutschen Nationalkökonomie* (The Errors of Historicism in German National Economy) had charged that Schmoller and the Historical School of Political Economy, through their reliance on a descriptive presentation of their findings, had avoided formulating the clear concepts necessary to a scientific approach. Otto Hintze, who in his studies of the Prussian silk industry and the Prussian administration came from the Schmoller school, and Max Weber, who began his work as a legal scholar and economist before he turned to sociology, attempted to introduce into empirical study the conceptual rigor that was lacking in the work of the Schmoller school. In an important article on Lamprecht in the *Historische Zeitschrift*, Otto Hintze in 1897 took a mediating position in the Lamprecht controversy.[3] While the critics of Lamprecht's *Deutsche Geschichte* often referred to Wilhelm Windelband's distinction between the individualizing concepts of the human sciences and the generalizing concepts of the natural sciences, Hintze emphasized that history is concerned with both individual and collective phenomena and that the latter require abstract, analytical concepts in order to be understood. Max Weber in an important essay in 1904[4] criticized Knies, Roscher, and Schmoller, the representatives of the Historical School of National Economy, on grounds similar to those on which Menger had criticized them, for proceeding descriptively without a clearly defined set of concepts to guide their inquiry. Hintze and Weber agreed with classical historicism, however, that every society was held together by a set of attitudes and values that needed to be understood in order to comprehend the unique character of the society. Hence Weber called for a *"verstehende Soziologie,"* a sociology that aimed at "understanding" the society and culture it studied. But for Weber understanding did not mean the same thing that it had for Ranke, Droysen, and

Dilthey, primarily an intuitive act of empathy or direct experience, but a highly rational process. "Understanding" (*Verstehen*) by no means excluded causal "explanation" (*Erklärung*) or analysis.

For Weber, but also for Hintze, the difference between sociology and history was not as great as it was for classical historicism. In its beginnings in France and America sociology often operated with ahistorical typologies, while history preferred a narrative form of discourse that kept abstractions at a minimum. Hintze and Weber viewed sociology much more historically than Durkheim, but at the same time they viewed history much more sociologically than the great majority of historians. In his great essays in the 1920s on feudalism and capitalism as historical categories,[5] Hintze attempted to formulate abstract concepts, which he considered to be the prerequisites of scientific thought, but then proceeded to fill them with a concrete historical content. Much more detached than the German historical school, including not only Ranke but also the historical economists such as Schmoller, Hintze denied the notion dear to the German tradition that the state constituted a "moral" or "spiritual" entity. Instead he saw the state in empirical terms as merely one among many institutions (*Anstalt*) without an inherent claim to special dignity. Max Weber similarly rejected the apotheosis of the state and insisted on a "value free" science. Social science could analyze the value assumptions and practices of a society scientifically but it could not establish the validity of these values.

For Weber the questions a social scientist asks admittedly reflect the values he holds; in his actual research and findings, however, he must strive for objectivity and detachment. But science has to do not only with detachment but also with causal explanation. In the Neo-Kantian tradition, Weber denies that causality is anchored in objective reality, seeking it rather in the categories of scientific thought. The crucial element of scientific inquiry is thus contained in its methods. While every science is rooted within a definite culture, its methods possess a degree of validity and objectivity that transcends the limitations of the particular society or culture. Thus he observes: "For it is and will remain true that methodically correct proof in the social sciences, if it is to achieve its purpose, must be acknowledged as correct even by a Chinese, who, on the other hand, may be deaf to our conception of the ethical imperative."[6] Though Weber rejects Hegel's or Marx's view of history as a process leading to a rational society, he still believes that at least the history of the Western world since Hebrew and Greek antiquity is marked by an irrepressible process of "intellectualization" and "rationalization." The break with the historicist belief that there is continuity and coherence in history thus turns out to be no break at all, even if the optimistic faith of Condorcet, Hegel, or Marx that history leads to fulfillment, or of Ranke and Droysen that it has brought about an order in which men can live reasonably, is repudiated. Thus despite his pessimism and skepticism, Weber maintains key nineteenth-century notions regarding the coherence that marks history, or at least Western history. And although for him science and social science cannot ask philosophical or ethical questions, he continues to believe in the possibility of the "objective" character of scientific and social scientific inquiry, which follow a logic that has transcultural validity.

Chapter 4

American Traditions of Social History

While Marx and Weber took issue with the idealistic presuppositions of classical German historicism and their implications for historical studies and the social sciences, they maintained the historicist belief that the social sciences must proceed historically, and that history, despite ruptures, constitutes a continuous process with a high degree of coherence. The evolutionary conception of history and society also dominated much thought in the English-speaking world. But historical studies there drew on intellectual traditions reflective of a different social order than that of the continental European countries. Despite the high degree of industrialization in England and in the United States, at least in the public sector, bureaucratization was much less advanced than on the European continent. "Civil society," as it had been termed since the Scottish moral philosophers,[1] was much more independent of the state in English and American thought than in Hegel's or Ranke's conceptions of the body social. This openness was reflected in a much greater reluctance to seek large-scale explanations for events on the part of English and American historians and social scientists than among their colleagues in France and Germany.

As we saw, in America as in France, and in the case of Lamprecht in Germany, the discussion of methods around the turn of the century presupposed that traditional historical science at the universities no longer corresponded to the scientific and social requirements of a modern, democratic, industrial society. From this the participants in the discussions concluded that historical studies, which at the American universities too after 1870 had focused on politics, must be expanded to a broadly based history of society. In Germany, beginning with Wilhelm Riehl in the middle of the nineteenth century, an ethnographically oriented *Kulturgeschichte*, pursued largely outside the historical profession in local historical societies, had focused on the everyday life and customs of common people. But despite superficial similarities, the "New History" in the United States differed fundamentally from Riehl's kind of cultural history. While the latter looked back nostalgically to an idealized premodern agrarian society in which there were no significant social conflicts, the former affirmed modernity and along with it a democratic social order. While the older American "Scientific School," in its admiration of German scholarship, sought the roots of Anglo-Saxon America in the Germanic primeval past, the New Historians emphasized the breach with the premodern European past. For them America was a country of immigrants, who determined the character of the rural "frontier" in the West as well as that of the teeming cities in the East. A narrowly political history no longer sufficed. The sciences that interested the New Historians were those dealing with modern society, primarily economics and sociology, but also psychology. The faith in an American consensus, which had been so important for the older historiography, was now replaced by a new outlook, more aware of differences that divided the American population without denying the elements that contributed to a sense of national community.

It is difficult to reduce the New History to a common denominator. Charles Beard saw economic and social conflicts as the decisive factors in American history. James H. Robinson, Vernon Parrington, and Carl Becker emphasized the role of ideas, Perry Miller that of religion. Unreflected narration no longer sufficed. On the one hand, Turner, in his address to the American Historical Association in 1893, "Significance of the Frontier in American History,"[2] and Beard, in his *Economic Interpretation of the American Constitution* (1913), consciously formulated a historical problem that presupposed a theoretical framework. On the other hand, although the New Historians borrowed selectively from the various social sciences, they did not want to transform history into a systematic social science as Durkheim and Simiand in France and Marx, Lamprecht, and Max Weber in Germany had wanted to do. Their relationship to the social sciences was loose and eclectic, as it was for Henri Berr in France or Henri Pirenne[3] in Belgium. The New Historians were filled with optimism regarding the evolution of society toward a democratic goal, but they, along with Berr and Pirenne, were not seeking to discover laws of irreversible progress.

In the first two decades after World War II the political as well as the scientific assumptions of the "Progressive Historians," as the New Historians called themselves, were called into question. A new national consensus was discovered by American historians in the Cold War.[4] For them America appeared, in contrast to Europe, as a truly classless society, free of ideological divisions, which with the exception of the Civil War had been free of serious conflicts. And the Civil War, they held, would have been prevented had abolitionists and their radical opponents not introduced ideological fervor. They believed that an expansive capitalistic market economy had eliminated the final elements of class conflict. Daniel Bell in 1960 proclaimed the "end of ideology."[5] In those early years of the Cold War, American history and American society were increasingly held up as a model for the "free world." In their eyes, a society that had achieved industrial efficiency and created a mass consumer market required a history and a social science adequate to the realities of a modern world. For that, the computer appeared at the right time. Increasingly, quantifying methods were introduced into historical research not only in America, but also in England, France, Scandinavia, and elsewhere, even in the socialist countries. Quantification strengthened the claims of the social sciences to be scientific disciplines.

The application of quantitative methods to social phenomena does not, however, by itself signify the transition to a systematic, analytical social science. Often quantification is only an aid in buttressing arguments with statistical evidence. With developing computer technology, quantitative studies began to multiply in the fifties in the United States, but also elsewhere in several areas of research. In political history electoral behavior began to be correlated with social variables. Historical demography established itself as a quantitative discipline, especially in France and England. In the United States social mobility was examined with the help of the censuses that had been conducted every ten years since 1790. Finally, quantitative methods increasingly aided in the analysis of economic processes, though they could also be used in exploring aspects of culture, outlooks, attitudes, and patterns of behavior. Particularly in France and England, parish records were analyzed with the help of computers to reveal information about family constitution, births, marriages, deaths, and property, methods that became the basis of historical demography. Data on the age of marriage and on illegitimacy afforded insight into sexual behavior and thus information about the ideas of morality of the people included in the registers. In France the examination of thousands of wills yielded information about changing attitudes toward death and religion and thus about the extent of desecularization.

It is not suprising that quantitative studies became most firmly established in economic history. Both Marx and Weber had worked with an understanding of social science that on the one hand insisted on the use of clearly defined concepts and on the other took into consideration that, in the social in contrast to the natural sciences, these concepts must take into account the uniqueness as well as the comparability of societies and provide ways to explore the web of meanings and values that give these societies their coherence. They moreover recognized that the natural sciences too are products of human culture and can be understood only indirectly, by means of socially determined categories. In the final analysis, the social sciences deal with human relationships, which must be understood qualitatively, although quantitative data are useful in defining the contours of these relationships.

The highly quantitative research that played an important role in historical studies in the 1970s, especially in America and France, however, often presupposed a concept of science that historical studies could only satisfy if they formulated their findings in quantifiable language. Emmanuel Le Roy Ladurie commented in 1973 that "history that is not quantifiable cannot claim to be scientific."[6] This view had gained in importance in the 1960s and 1970s with the improvemements in computer technology and the resulting transformation of the economy. In his survey written in 1979 for UNESCO of trends in recent historical studies, Geoffrey Barraclough commented that "the search for quantity is beyond all doubt the most powerful of the new trends in history, the factor above all others which distinguishes historical attitudes in the 1970's from historical attitudes in the 1930's."[7] As I have suggested, we must distinguish here between, on the one hand, the occasional application of quantitative methods as they have been common in social and especially in economic history for many decades and, on the other, the conception of history as a hard science working with mathematical models. Between these two poles there emerged the orientation in America, and also in France and Scandinavia, that called itself "social science history." An example of the electronic processing of mass data was the gigantic "Philadelphia Social History Project," which set out to study the entire population of Philadelphia on the basis of several censuses of the nineteenth century in order to obtain precise information about social mobility. A not entirely dissimilar approach to social history was the *histoire sérielle* in France, which by means of mass data over long periods of time examined continuity and change not only in economic and social relations but also, as we shall see, in the study of mentalities.

Perhaps the most important advocates of a historiography that took the hard sciences as its models were the practitioners of the "New Economic History" in the United States. Proceeding from the assumptions of classical economics, the New Economic Historians worked with models of economic growth isolated from politics and society. Thus in their famous contrafactual study *Railroads and American Economic Growth*,[8] Robert Fogel and Douglass North, using exclusively economic data, posed the question of how the economy of the United States would have differed had the railroads not been developed. The New Economic History worked with four basic assumptions: (1) There are generally valid laws governing economic behavior, essentially corresponding to those formulated by Adam Smith and David Ricardo. These laws never operate unhampered, because political, ideological, religious, and other forces prevent them from doing so. Nevertheless, they represent a theoretical model of how the economy would function under ideal free market conditions. (2) The capitalist economy is characterized by constant growth, which, as Walt Rostow claimed in his *Stages of Economic Growth: A Non-Communist Manifesto*,[9] takes on similar forms in all modern and modernizing societies. Thus Marx's formulation, "The country which is industrially more developed only shows the less developed one the picture of its own future,"[10] also holds for Rostow. (Against this assumption Alexander Gerschenkron[11] argued that other countries began to industrialize later and under different political and social conditions than England and therefore were not fully comparable.) (3) The process of economic modernization necessarily leads to political modernization, that is, to a free market society and a liberal, parliamentarian democracy, as was demonstrated after World War II by the Western industrial nations. (4) The quantitative method can be applied not only to economic but also to social processes.

In 1974 Fogel and Stanley Engerman's computer-based study of slavery in the American South appeared.[12] As the authors wrote in the preface, they not only wanted to answer once and for all the controversial question about the profitability of slavery, but on the basis of quantifiable sources to offer irrefutable information about the quality of the material life of the slaves and beyond this about their family life and their work ethic. The book, which at first was widely welcomed in the American press as a convincing scientific work, was very soon subjected to a devastating critique by both conventional social historians and economic historians, who understood how difficult it is to transform qualitative evidence into quantitative statements.[13] This did not prevent Fogel from being called to an endowed chair at Harvard University and in 1994, together with Douglass North, to receive the Nobel Prize for Economics. The historical science rejected by Fogel was in his mind distinguished from other social sciences in its continuing reliance on a mode of discourse largely free of technical language and therefore accessible to an educated reading public. For Fogel this was irreconcilable with true science; historians, as all scientists, must be technically trained specialists who communicate in the language of formal science with other specialists.[14] Fogel, despite his insistence on the objective, value-free character of historical science—not unlike Ranke, who also stressed the impartiality and objectivity of the historian—proceeded from assumptions that were by no means value free. In Fogel's case, his identification with an existing growth- and consumption-oriented economy led him to insufficiently consider the dangers inherent in this economy.

II

The Middle Phase: The Challenge of the Social Sciences

Chapter 5

France: The *Annales*

The French *Annales* school of historians, centered around the journal *Annales*, occupy a unique place in the historiography of the twentieth century. On the one hand, their writers share the confidence of other social science-oriented historians in the possibility of scientific approaches to history; on the other hand, they are aware of the limits of such approaches. In the course of more than eight decades they have profoundly changed conceptions of what constitutes and who makes history. They have offered a very different conception of historical time from that held by most historians in the nineteenth and twentieth centuries. Virtually all historians from Ranke to Marx and Weber, and after them the American social science-oriented historians, had seen history in terms of movement across a one-dimensional time from the past to the future. The *Annales* historians radically modified this conception by stressing the relativity and multilayering of time.

Annales historians have insisted that they do not represent a "school," though they have often been identified as such, but rather a spirit marked by openness to new methods and approaches to historical research.[1] To a very large extent they are right. The publications by members of the circle reflect very different interests and approaches. They have not formulated an explicit theory or philosophy of history; in fact, research has always taken precedence over theoretical reflection. Their historical writings nevertheless reflect theoretical presuppositions.

Despite their protestation that they are not a school, the *Annales* since the end of World War II have had a firm institutional basis. And despite fundamental changes over time, there have been continuities in the language they have used and the concepts they have employed since the early works of their founders, Lucien Febvre and Marc Bloch.[2] The discussions about methods that, beginning in 1900, took place in Henri Berr's journal, *Revue de synthèse historique*, mentioned earlier, are part of the prehistory of the *Annales*. Lucien Febvre's book about the Franche-Comté, also mentioned above, signals the transition to a new kind of historical science. In it the entities that up to that point had played such an important role—the state, but also the economy, religion, law, literature, and the arts—lose their autonomy and are integrated into an all-embracing culture. Culture is no longer understood as the privileged intellectual and aesthetic domain of an elite, but rather as the way in which a whole population experiences and lives life.

Lucien Febvre and especially Marc Bloch, who studied in Leipzig and Berlin between 1908 and 1909, closely followed the work being done in social and economic history in Germany. There are parallels between Febvre's book about the Franche-Comté and Lamprecht's earlier economic history of the Moselle valley in the middle ages, although probably no direct influence. While economic and social history in Germany focused on administrative and constitutional aspects, Lamprecht and Febvre were concerned with the close ties between social, economic, and political structures and the patterns of thought and behavior in a specific geographic, cultural region. Febvre's interests reflected a training different from that of most German historians. In Germany, of 141 occupants of university history chairs in the period from 1850 to 1900, 87 had studied philology as a secondary field and of these 72 had specialized in classical philology; 23 had studied theology or philosophy, only 10 economics, and 12 geography. In contrast, in France geography was an integral part of the *agrégation*, the examination required for a university career.[3] Moreover, geography as it had emerged in France as an academic discipline in the late nineteenth century under the guidance of Paul Vidal de la Blache, who had been deeply influenced by Carl Ritter and the German tradition of geography, also was historical and cultural in its orientation. Vidal de la Blache's *géographie humaine*, which avoided the geographic determinism of his contemporary Friedrich Ratzel in Germany, deeply influenced the entire tradition of *Annales* historians from Febvre onward. In addition to geography, there was Durkheim's sociological approach, interpreted for the *Annales* historians by his student, the economist François Simiand. Durkheim on the one hand wanted to transform sociology into a strict science, which for Simiand involved mathematical formulations.[4] On the other hand, consciousness, perceived as collective consciousness, was for Durkheim the central subject of the science of society, of which norms, customs, and religion were important components. The acceptance of these scholarly approaches reflects the close links between geography, economics, and anthropology in French historiography, in contrast with the emphasis on the state, administration, and jurisprudence of the German tradition that included Max Weber. In this light the great importance Febvre and Bloch attributed to anonymous structures becomes understandable, as well as the attention they paid to the aspects of feelings and experience embedded in the collective mentalities that form the subject of historical anthropology.

The intellectual bases of the *Annales* were laid by Febvre and Bloch long before they founded the journal. Febvre's *Philippe II et la Franche-Comté* (1911) and Marc Bloch's *The Royal Touch* (1924),[5] on the magic arts of healing of the French and English kings in the Middle Ages, appeared before the founding of the journal in 1929, as did Febvre's *Martin Luther: A Destiny*.[6] The *Annales* at no point stood for a closely defined doctrine. In part patterning its name on the *Vierteljahrschrift für Sozial- und Wirtschaftsgeschichte*, the oldest and still very much respected journal in the field, the new journal originally called itself *Annales d'histoire économique et sociale*; although from the beginning it perceived itself very differently from the *Vierteljahrschrift*.[7] After 1946 the title was changed to *Annales. Economies. Sociétés. Civilisations*, in order to emphasize its interdisciplinary character more strongly. History for the *Annales* historians occupied a central role among the sciences dealing with man, but in a different way than it had for classical historicism. While the latter had elevated the state as the key institution to which all other aspects of society and culture were subordinated, *Annales* historians abolished the boundaries between the traditional disciplines in order to integrate them into the "sciences of man" (*sciences de l'homme*). The plural was used intentionally, in order to emphasize the plurality of sciences. The *Annales*, not following the models provided by Ranke's fragmentary or Droysen's systematic dogmatic pronouncements,[8] formulated no theory of history or historiography, not even in Bloch's *The Historian's Craft*[9]—notes he jotted down at the front in 1940. The purpose of the *Annales* was, as Bloch and Febvre explained in the introduction to the first issue of the journal, to provide a forum for various directions and new approaches.[10]

Also no clear common political denominator can be found in the *Annales*. Although its contributors were overwhelmingly republicans and French patriots, they were much less ideological than the bulk of German historians, who saw a primary function of their scholarship to be the justification of German national aims and of the political and social institutions of Imperial Germany. It is, however, important to understand the political engagement of the founders of the *Annales*, and to remember that Marc Bloch, who was of Jewish descent, was tortured and murdered by the Germans in 1944 as a resistance fighter. As for the role of the *Annales* in the French academic scene, Febvre and Bloch, until they were called to Paris in 1933 and 1936 respectively,[11] were at the University of Strasbourg, and it was from here that they pursued their conflict with Seignobos and the traditional political historians at the Sorbonne. Later, things were very different. If they had occupied a somewhat marginal position in the 1930s, Febvre and the *Annales* in fact became the establishment after the war, when a new interest in cultural and social history arose and a critical reconsideration took place of the attitudes that Bloch, in *The Strange Defeat*,[12] charged had helped to pave the way for the catastrophe of 1940.

In 1946 the Annales received a firm institutional basis in the newly formed Sixth Section of the Ecole Pratique des Hautes Etudes. As noted, the Ecole had been founded in 1868 as a research center according to the German model. Lacking the normal courses of study, it was dedicated exclusively to research and to the training of researchers. In the Fourth Section, devoted to historical studies, seminars following Ranke's pattern were introduced. The Sixth Section, reorganized in 1972 as the Ecole des Hautes Etudes en Sciences Sociales (EHESS), was committed to integrating history and the social science disciplines within a comprehensive "science of man" (*science de l'homme*), which would include not only the traditional social sciences so important in the early years of the *Annales*, namely economics, sociology, and anthropology, but also linguistics, semiotics, the sciences of literature and the arts, and psychoanalysis. Through the funding the Ecole received from the French National Council for Scientific Research (CNRS) and from American foundations, it was able to exert a major influence on research in France.

This institutionalization had conflicting results. It favored interdisciplinary research and thus, often, a new openness, and it made teamwork possible, coordinating various projects that increasingly used the new technological means of data processing. Thus in the sixties and seventies, on the one hand the great syntheses of Fernand Braudel, Pierre Goubert, Jacques Le Goff, Georges Duby, Emmanuel Le Roy Ladurie, and Robert Mandrou appeared in the *Annales*; on the other hand were highly specialized contributions, frequently written in a jargon incomprehensible to outsiders.

In spite of the great variety of methodological and conceptual approaches in the now over eighty years since Febvre's book about the Franche-Comté appeared in 1911, the works of *Annales* historians have had much in common. To illustrate this we shall briefly look at several of the important works that appeared between 1911 and the 1980s: Febvre, *Philippe II et la Franche Comté* (1911); Bloch, *Feudal Society* (1939–40);[13] Febvre, *The Problem of Unbelief in the Sixteenth Century: The Religion of Rabelais* (1942);[14] Fernand Braudel, *The Mediterranean and the Mediterranean World in the Age of Philip II* (1949);[15] Emmanuel Le Roy Ladurie, *Peasants of Languedoc* (1966)[16] and *Montaillou* (1975);[17] and finally Braudel, *Civilization and Capitalism: 15th to 19th Century* (1979–87)[18] and *The Identity of France* (1986).[19]

It is striking that in none of these works is there a central institution serving as a guiding thread in a historical narrative in which the actions of persons play a decisive role. This does not mean that the role of politics is ignored. In Bloch's examination of feudal society it plays an essential role, but in a different way than in German studies. While the latter focus on the formal aspects of feudalism, on political, ecclesiastical, and juridical institutions, Bloch approaches feudalism anthropologically as a complex of interpersonal relations. In using the term "complex" I intentionally avoid the word "system," rarely used by the *Annales* historians and seen by them as objectifying and reifying human behavior far too much. For the same reason one must be careful with the concept "structure," which is used by the *Annales* historians. To be sure their stress is on structures. Individuals, who occupy a key position in nineteenth-century historiography, are mentioned rarely, if at all in these works. In Bloch's *Feudal Society*, for example, the kings appear rarely and only marginally. In Braudel's book on the Mediterranean, they are relegated to the separate section on the political history of the region with little organic connection to the two preceding sections dealing with the almost timeless geographical setting of the Mediterranean region and its slowly changing economic and social structure. Individuals reappear in Le Roy Ladurie's early-fourteenth-century village of heretics, Montaillou, the focus of a foray into historical anthropology in which a set of narratives portrays men and women embedded in an age-old folk culture.

As I have noted, the *Annales* historians introduced a new concept of historical time. Their studies, including Febvre's *Philippe II et la Franche Comté* and *The Problem of Unbelief in the Sixteenth Century: The Religion of Rabelais*, Bloch's *Feudal Society*, Braudel's Mediterranean book, and Ladurie's *Montaillou*, are more concerned with viewing a culture or an age apart from the stream of history than with relating a process of change through the ages. The historians we have discussed have largely abandoned the idea of a linear, directional history, characteristic of much of historical thought since the period Reinhart Koselleck has described as the transition between about 1750 and 1850 from the premodern to the modern time.[20] Michel Foucault considers the idea of *one* history to be an invention of modern times, which have already ended. Most *Annales* historians would concur. In the place of one historical time, they see a plurality of coexisting times, not only among different civilizations but also within each civilization. This idea is most clearly developed in the structure of Braudel's Mediterranean book, which distinguishes three different times, each with its own speed: the almost stationary time of the Mediterranean as a geographic space (*longue durée*), the slow time of changes in social and economic structures (*conjonctures*), and the fast time of political events (*événements*). On this basis Jacques Le Goff wrote his classic essay "Merchant's Time and Church's Time in the Middle Ages."[21]

With the abandonment of the concept of linear time, the confidence in progress and with it the faith in the superiority of Western culture also break down. There no longer exists a concept of unified historical development on which a grand narrative of the history of man can be based. Moreover, historical narrative must find new forms of expression under these new conditions. As in the novel, so in history, the story with a central plot in which individuals take their place as free agents disappears. And the nation, which provided the sense of identity for broad segments of the population in the nineteenth century and well into the twentieth, is largely absent from these works. With few exceptions, the historiography of the *Annales* is either regional or supranational. The regions often assume a certain unity, not only in Febvre's book on the Franche-Comté but also in a host of studies in the 1960s that rely heavily on demographic data.[22] Braudel's Mediterranean book deals with the whole Mediterranean world, Christian and Moslem. His *Structures of Everyday Life* (1967)[23] deals with material aspects of life—the emergence of capitalist institutions as well as the various tangible aspects of life from health to food and fashions—in the period from 1500 to 1800, focusing on Europe but within a broadly comparative framework encompassing the entire world. Braudel's last great work, *The Identity of France* (1987), returns to national history but defines France not from the center in Paris but in terms of a pluralism of regions whose particular identity has remained stable throughout the centuries. Again the stress is not on change but on the *longue durée*, the persistence of a peasant culture and mentality into the twentieth century.

These remarks should not give the impression that the *Annales* outlook remained constant over eighty years, although there is a continuity between the early works of Febvre and Bloch and those of the later *Annales*. They reflect the most important transformations in the historical thinking of the twentieth century, but they have given these their own character. Since they have exerted important influences on historical writing worldwide they have in turn contributed to changes in historical perspective. One can distinguish perhaps four different phases of *Annales* historiography, reflecting the four generations of historians since Febvre's early work, but it must be kept in mind that historians in each generation have undergone changes in outlook that reflect the changes in the intellectual environment in which they have worked. Thus Febvre's early work shows similarities with French and German attempts to write an integrated social and economic history of a geographic, historical region that does not ignore political aspects. Geography is an important segment of *Annales* historiography, but it is always a "human geography" aware of the interaction of culture and physical space. Bloch's *French Rural History* (1931),[24] for example, in which he seeks to reconstruct patterns of land use in the Middle Ages and the cultural consequences that resulted from them and are evident in aerial photography, introduces a focus on material factors. Remarkable in many of the *Annales* works is the great attention given to religious phenomena, again generally seen anthropologically as part of a collective mentality. The interest in religious thinkers at the turn to the modern age is particularly pronounced in Febvre's preoccupation with Luther's belief and Rabelais's supposed unbelief. The French tradition of cultural anthroplogy from Marcel Mauss and Lévi-Bruhl to Lévi-Strauss plays an increasing role in Febvre's thought, along with the new linguistic and semiotic approaches. The question of unbelief in the sixteenth century is for Febvre not primarily one of the ideas Rabelais or other individuals articulated but rather one of the "mental tools" with which they operated, of which their language is the chief one. Febvre's study thus takes on archeological aspects. Language here is less the conscious creation of the men and women who speak it than an interrelated system of meanings into which each generation is born and which shapes its thought processes.

In this sense language, too, is part of the material world. Yet the materialism of Febvre and Bloch is far removed from that of Marx. Marx's philosophy of history still shares the speculative aspects of much of nineteenth-century philosophy of history. When Bloch is concerned with technology, whether the water-mill or the plough,[25] he sees the tools with which people work in a certain society as keys to their ways of thinking and living. Much more important than economics for the analysis of a society or a culture is semiotics, because, as Bloch showed in *The Royal Touch* (1924) and in *Feudal Society* and Febvre in his Rabelais book, every culture is a system of meanings that expresses itself in language and symbolism. Febvre himself reflected the changes that took place in the intellectual climate during his life. His Rabelais book, with its strong semiotic orientation, could not have been written three decades earlier at the time when his Franche-Comté work appeared in 1911, a work that still reflected the much more transparent world of social and economic history of the turn of the century.

In comparison with Bloch and Febvre, Braudel's work seems much less subtle. The idea that the external world, understood as climate, biology, and technology, sets sharp limits to what men and women can do is much more pervasive throughout his work than in that of Febvre and Bloch. The basic significance of the *longue durée* is that there is little change over the ages in the aspects of life that matter. Of course, Braudel does not deny the impact of tastes, ideas, and attitudes. Hence his interest in housing, clothing, and food as elements not just of material subsistence but of material culture as expressed in architecture, interior decoration, fashion, and cuisine. Braudel paves the way for the quantitative history of the 1960s and 1970s without himself becoming a quantifier. In his economic history of France, which he wrote together with the economic historian Ernest Labrousse,[26] he is interested in the great recurrent cycles that determine economic activity over decades and centuries. Economics thus becomes a hard science, closer to that of the classical political economists than to the German school, but without the former's belief in the persistence and the desirability of growth.

In the 1960s the general fascination in the social sciences with quantification also takes over the *Annales*. *Annales* historians increasingly want to be scientists. They often call their institutes "laboratories" and speak of history as a science, a social science to be sure, but nevertheless one that, as they repeat, must work quantitatively if it is to be scientific.[27] A broad segment of French social history in the 1960s depended heavily on quantification, as for instance the demographic studies already mentioned, which on the basis of mass demographic data sought to present a "total history" (*histoire totale*) of a region. Starting with statistical data reconstructed from parish records on regenerative behavior, these studies approached the broader questions of sexual attitudes. Perhaps the most ambitious quantitative study of the 1960s was Le Roy Ladurie's *Peasants of Languedoc* (1966). For long stretches this was a "history without people,"[28] a statistical analysis of the interrelation of long cycles of population growth and food prices informed by Malthusian assumptions. It appeared in the same year as his history of climate since the year 1000,[29] reconstructed in part on the hard material evidence of tree rings.

But the *Peasants of Languedoc* paradoxically also marked a departure from a "history without people," a formulation of Le Roy Ladurie, toward a new history of consciousness. The history of consciousness always occupied an important place in *Annales* writings. *Feudal Society*, too, in basic ways had been a history of consciousness, in which a social system was analyzed in the ways in which it expressed itself in attitudes and outlooks. Philippe Ariès, in his *Centuries of Childhood* (1960)[30] and *The Hour of Our Death* (1981),[31] explored the history of mentalities in early modern Europe, relying on literary and artistic sources. Thus a history of mentalities was launched among historians of the third *Annales* generation, preeminently Robert Mandrou, Jacques Le Goff, and Georges Duby, who explored popular attitudes in a social and economic context. Mandrou dealt with witchcraft and the early capitalistic mindset of the Fuggers,[32] Le Goff[33] and Duby[34] with broad segments of medieval religious, commercial, and military life. Similarly, art and literature became important sources for the reconstruction of past mentalities, as they had been for Bloch. The fascination with the computer transformed the study of mentalities. Indeed, the "history of mentalities" as it was pursued by Pierre Chaunu[35] and Michel Vovelle[36] proceeded from the assumption that the reconstruction of mentalities was possible only on the basis of the analysis of mass data such as wills, which yielded information on views of death and religion. In this turn to quantification, *Annales* historians did not point out new directions but took their place in what had become a broad movement in historical social science research. Quantification was not the child of the *Annales*, but it had a good basis in *Annales* traditions stressing the material basis of culture. These same traditions, however, in their anthropological approach also pointed in the direction of a history of consciousness, which was open to the existential, experiential aspects of life. The *Peasants of Languedoc* was a high point in quantitative history employing theoretical models. At the same time it contains a dramatic narrative reconstruction of the massacre of Catholics by Protestants in the Carneval of Romans in 1580, explained in part by demographic and economic pressures between a Protestant burgher class and the impoverished peasant and journeymen's classes, but fought out in highly aggressive symbolic actions with sexual overtones that could only be understood psychoanalytically. Demography and economics were now replaced or at least buttressed by semiotics and depth psychology. The pressure for a history of the existential experiences of concrete human beings, and the resulting critical attitude toward a social science history that concentrated on structures and processes, found expression in the discovery by *Annales* historians of the history of everyday life. Le Roy Ladurie's *Peasants of Languedoc* was followed only nine years later by his *Montaillou* (1975), which, on the basis of the testimony of the peasants of a village in Southern France who in the early fourteenth century were investigated by the Inquisition on the suspicion of heresy, tries to reconstruct the most intimate and personal details and thoughts of common people.

The third generation of *Annales* historians is now approaching or already in retirement, having participated in the general enthusiasm for hard quantitative social science and then, as in the case of Le Roy Ladurie, turned to historical anthropology. A fourth generation, including Jacques Revel, André Burguière, and Bernard Lepetit, has noted the dissolution of a specific *Annales* orientation into a historiography that is going in a variety of directions. Indicative of the changes taking place in the *Annales* is the change in the title of the journal in 1994, the replacement of the old subtitle, *Economies. Sociétés. Civilisation,* by *Histoire, Sciences Sociales.* While the former subtitle had stressed the comprehensive interests of the *Annales*, it had reflected a bias against political history. This bias also included a preference for simpler, premodern societies, in which ethnological methods were better applicable than in complex industrial or postindustrial ones.

It has in fact often been held against the *Annales* that they were unable to deal with modern times. Undoubtedly the focus of *Annales* historiography has been on the Middle Ages and the Ancien Regime, but the *Annales* have never entirely neglected the modern period. In the 1930s they devoted much space to the problems of modern industrial society in the large cities both in the developed and in the then still colonial world.[37] Articles dealt with fascism, bolshevism, and the New Deal, but surprisingly not with Nazism. Bloch's *The Strange Defeat* was a critical coming to terms with the Third Republic. Several very important studies on nineteenth-century French society appeared in the 1950s and 1960s, including Adeline Daumard's *La Bourgeoisie parisienne de 1815–1848,*[38] Jean Bouvier's *Crédit Lyonnais de 1863 à 1882,*[39] Charles Morazé's *The Triumph of the Bourgeoisie,*[40] and Louis Chevalier, *Classes labourieuses et classes dangéreuses à Paris pendant la première moitié du XIXe siècle,*[41] the last outside the circle of the *Annales.* The primacy of economic and sociological categories in these works was replaced by the strongly anthropological concerns of Maurice Agulhon[42] and Mona Ozouf,[43] who examined the republican traditions of nineteenth-century France through its symbols. Over a period of several decades, Marc Ferro devoted himself to the twentieth century in his studies of World War I[44] and of Bolshevik Russia.[45] François Furet since the mid-1970s has turned to a history of the French Revolution that rejects Marxist categories of class and stresses politics, ideas, and culture.[46]

What remains distinctive of *Annales* writings on the modern and contemporary world is their focus on culture and symbols to make modern political traditions comprehensible, as in the volumes of *Les Lieux des mémoires* (1984–86),[47] a collaborative work on the symbols, monuments, and shrines of modern French national consciousness. Although the *Annales* have remained a movement deeply rooted in French traditions of scholarship, perhaps no scholarly movement in the twentieth century has had such an impact internationally as a model for new paths of historical investigation of culture and society. Their influence extended even to the socialist countries, where historians realized increasingly that the *Annales* offered much better access to material culture and to the everyday life of common people than did dogmatic Marxism. Thus in 1971 there appeared in the Soviet Union Aaron Gurevich's synthesis, *Categories of Medieval Culture*,[48] which avoided Marxist language and schemes of history and built on the tradition of Marc Bloch. Nor was Gurevich alone; in the 1980s a small but significant circle of *Annales* historians began to form in the Soviet Union. In Poland, where basic works of Bloch, Febvre, and Braudel were translated as early as the 1970s, the impact of the *Annales* was even greater.[49] The *Annales* in turn published contributions by the most important Polish economic and cultural historians. Undoubtedly contributing to their influence was the fact that *Annales* historians on the one hand were committed to what they understood as a scientific approach to the historical past, and on the other worked with conceptions of history and society that were much more comprehensive and open than those of other social science-oriented historiography in the West or of official Marxism in the East.

The complexity and pluralism in their approaches, however, also gave rise to serious contradictions in their practice. Thus, as we saw, especially in the three decades after the end of World War II, many historians in the *Annales* circle were fascinated by social science approaches that promised firm, objective knowledge. Braudel's emphasis on long enduring structures and on the material foundations of culture were not free of this scientism. Yet, as we also saw, there was a firmly established tradition, extending from Bloch and Febvre to Le Goff, Duby, and to the present, that relied heavily on such sources as art, folklore, and customs and therefore encouraged more subtle, qualitative ways of thinking. The works of these historians helped to bridge the gap between history and literature. Their strongly anthropological note prevented the main currents of *Annales* historiography from succumbing to the scientism that characterized much social science thought. The *Annales* throughout their history have been remarkably free of confidence in the superior qualities of a Western civilization built on scientific and technological skills, and free of the concepts of modernization so central to much social science theory. On the contrary, they have focused intensely on a premodern world. Perhaps this helps to explain the sudden interest internationally in the *Annales* after 1970, at a time when the basic assumptions of social science history began to be questioned.

Chapter 6

Critical Theory and Social History: "Historical Social Science" in the Federal Republic of Germany

The sharp distinction made by Lawrence Stone in 1978[1] between an analytical social science that seeks coherent explanations and a narrative history that seeks to understand the intentions and actions of men and women by embedding them in a story is much less applicable to historical writing in continental Europe. Here, too, we witnessed a burgeoning of social science orientations in the 1950s and 1960s, but conceptions of social science remained much more concerned with culture than with economic models. This is true even now and, as we shall see, even of recent Marxist historiography. Perhaps at no time since the Enlightenment have theoretical discussions bridged national lines so much as in the last three decades; nor have historians in various Western countries been so aware of each other's work. Yet despite their international character, these discussions reflect differences in national cultures and historiographical traditions.

Historical studies in Germany in the 1960s cannot be understood without taking into consideration two factors: (1) the intellectual heritage of social science thought in Germany, with its roots in classical German culture and Idealist philosophy; and (2) the catastrophic course of German politics in the first half of the twentieth century. Very much as in other countries, historians in Germany, or at least in its Western part, in the 1960s and 1970s turned increasingly to social science models and in the 1980s became wary of them. But there were significant differences. While in France, the United States, Italy, Poland, and elsewhere the importance of the social sciences for historical research had been well established by the 1960s, many German historians still clung to older traditions of scholarship and historical thought that resisted innovation. Reasons for this lay in part in Germany's political history, in her painful and belated democratization. Moreover, history had become a professional discipline in Germany in the first half of the nineteenth century, before industrialization with its social consequences made itself felt, as we have already noted. Patterns of historical thought reflecting realities of a preindustrial and predemocratic age remained firmly established in German academic institutions in the last third of the century, when the modern discipline of history was being introduced in other countries. The course of German history after the failure of the 1848 revolution, and the subsequent surrender by German historians of their liberal convictions during the process of German unification under Bismarck, had reinforced their emphasis on the centralility of the state and on international affairs at the expense of a history of society. As we saw, social history was viewed with suspicion in Germany and often identified with Marxism. Thus, at the turn of the century, when historians in France, Belgium, the United States, and elsewhere were turning to the social sciences to broaden their historical understanding of a modern, industrial, and democratic society—in America particularly to economics, sociology, and psychology; in France to these same emerging disciplines but also to human geography and anthropology—the German historical profession almost to a man resisted such innovation. Social history was largely confined to the economics departments, which in Germany maintained a stronger historical focus than in the English-speaking countries or in Austria. This opposition to social history and social sciences persisted in the Weimar Republic, where historians who had been trained and politically socialized before 1914 nostalgically looked back to the Hohenzollern monarchy,[2] and it continued well into the 1960s.

The intense interest in the social sciences in the West Germany of the 1960s on the part of a younger generation of historians, born toward the end of the Weimar Republic, or even after 1933, but trained academically after 1945, was closely linked to their eagerness to confront the German past critically and their commitment to a democratic society. For them, the question of how the Nazi dictatorship in all its barbarity was possible was central to an understanding of modern German history. In contrast to France, where historians in the *Annales* tradition preferred to deal with a premodern, preindustrial world, most frequently with the politics left out, the new generation of German social historians placed politics in the center of their studies, but unlike their older colleagues linked politics closely to social forces and problems of modernization. They also worked in a tradition of social science that was deeply influenced by Max Weber's political sociology, and through Weber by Marx, and was sensitive to the close interrelation of politics and society.

An important point of departure for the critical discussions of the German past in the Federal Republic was Fritz Fischer's *Germany's War Aims in the First War,*[3] published in 1961. Fritz Fischer (born 1908) belonged to an older generation, trained in the Weimar Republic, that had pursued traditional historical interests. In fact, as a young scholar he had written for Walter Frank's Nazi Reichsinstitut für Geschichte des Neuen Deutschlands.[4] However, Fischer's book represented a radical break with the conventional interpretation of modern German history. Although in its reliance on government sources it was methodologically conventional, its conclusions were not. On the basis of these sources, Fischer concluded that the Imperial government in the summer of 1914 had consciously risked a preventive war. The government had yielded to a broad consensus among economic interest groups, from industry and agriculture to the labor unions, that favored extension of German political and economic hegemony over much of Europe, particularly the East, and supplanting of Great Britain and France as the major colonial powers. Fischer realized that, to substantiate his claim of close interaction between economic pressure groups and the political leadership, subsequent research would have to extend its scope beyond archival research on decision making, which he had already done, to more broadly examine the structural framework within which these decisions were made. He raised the question of the continuity of German expansionist policies from the Wilhelminian to the Nazi period, which raised the further question: to what extent must German imperialism be understood within the framework of German institutions going back to the nineteenth century?

Fischer was not alone in asking these questions. Historians such as Arthur Rosenberg, Hans Rosenberg, and Hajo Holborn, who had begun their careers in the Weimar Republic and been forced to emigrate in 1933, had asked them before. A younger generation now took up these ideas in the 1960s. Important to their discussion was the publication of Eckart Kehr's essays from the late Weimar period[5] by Hans Ulrich Wehler in 1965 and the republication in 1966 of Kehr's doctoral dissertation *Schlachtflottenbau und Parteipolitik 1894–1901: Versuch eines Querschnitts durch die innenpolitischen, sozialen und ideologischen Voraussetzungen des deutschen Imperialismus*,[6] first published in 1930. Kehr had argued in his dissertation that the Imperial government's decision in the 1890s to enter the naval race was motivated not by considerations of national security but by domestic political and social pressures that sought to maintain the power base of the industrial and agrarian elites against democratization and social reforms. Both Kehr and Wehler saw German industrialization as having been shaped by the authoritarian framework of Imperial Germany within which it had taken place, the values and ideals of which belonged to an older preindustrial society and culture. They went on from here to contend that the German policies that led to World War I resulted from the contradictions between economic and social modernization on the one hand and political backwardness on the other.

For both Kehr and Wehler historical studies served as a means to critically examine the German national past. Wehler in his writings of the late 1960s and 1970s, in which he sought to lay the foundations for a "Historical Social Science," developed a conception of social science closely linked to the "Critical Theory" of the Frankfurt School (Max Horkheimer and Theodor Adorno), indebted to Marx but freed of the speculative and authoritarian aspects of Marxist doctrine. Wehler challenged

Max Weber's imperative of value neutrality in social science research, a postulate that Weber himself, as a highly political scholar, violated in practice. Although Wehler, in contrast to Kehr, distanced himself emphatically from Marx, he assumed that the development of German society was determined by the persistence of structural and social inequalities. Like Kehr, however, he rejected Marx's notion of the primacy of economic forces and replaced it with the Weberian conception of "politics [*Herrschaft*], economics, and culture" as the three interrelated forces that determine every society.[7]

In sharp contrast to the critique of modernity that prevailed in the Western historiography of the 1960s, Wehler viewed the process of modernization, which he considered irrepressible, positively, and did so more hopefully than Weber did, who was very much aware of the contradictory qualities of this process. For Wehler the catastrophic course of modern German history had its roots in the incomplete modernization of Germany. He thus remarked that his assessment of the course of German history rests on the assumption that "the progressive economic modernization of German society should have been accompanied by a modernization of social relations and politics. Industrialization with its permanent technological revolution should have brought with it a development in the direction of a society of legally free and politically responsible citizens capable of making their own decisions," which in the German case it clearly did not.[8]

This conception of a "separate [German] path" (*Sonderweg*) to modernity has been severely criticized[9] because in the eyes of its critics it not only oversimplifies the political and social development of the West in general and of Germany in particular but fails to recognize that there is no one path to modernity. The crucial element in Wehler's conception of modernization, however, consists in his political message, his repudiation of German autocratic traditions and his affirmation of West Germany's assumption after 1945 of the democratic heritage of the West and specifically of a social democracy that combines political democracy with a profound sense of social responsibility.

Wehler's research and that of the social historians close to him in the so-called "Bielefeld School"—not actually a school but a circle of like-minded historians of whom several were at the

University of Bielefeld—proceeds from two basic assumptions. The first is that history should assume the form of a social science, but of a historical social science (*Historische Sozialwissenschaft*) as Wehler calls it,[10] which, unlike the behavioral social sciences in the American tradition, approaches society with clearly formulated questions related to social change. The second is that there is a close connection between scientific research and social practice. Wehler's conception of historical social science takes for granted Weber's broadening of Marx's concept of social formations, by which it is possible to understand a society and an epoch as a whole that is determined by political and sociocultural as well as by economic factors. He further accepts Marx's assumption that the history of the West can be understood as a continuous, unitary process since its prehistorical origins. Social history, or, as Wehler prefers to call it, historical social science, thus encompasses social, political, economic, and also sociocultural and intellectual phenomena in the broadest sense. The central theme of historical studies is the progressive transformation of social structures.

At the same time Wehler believes that the historian has a political responsibility. He sees this responsibility through the categories of Critical Theory as interpreted by Max Horkheimer and more recently by Jürgen Habermas; that is, he sees it in terms of a society toward which our intellectual efforts must strive, one that will be organized along reasonable (*vernünftig*), humane lines that allow humans to live in dignity as autonomous beings able to participate in the shaping of their destinies. This ideal, with its roots in the Enlightenment, serves for Wehler as a criterion for the critical examination of past and present societies. Wehler's idea of modernization is thus at its base normative: history must become not only a social science but a critical social science. It affirms modernization as a process of permanent transformation in which science and technology develop hand in hand with increasing freedom, political maturity, and responsibility among a society's members. For Wehler it should be the main task of German social historians to ask why modernization occurred differently in Germany than in other Western European countries or in North America, leading to the disastrous consequences of the period from 1933 to 1945.

Thus, as the values of a modern society that combined industrial society with social democracy were coming under widespread scrutiny in the West, these same values were being broadly affirmed by a considerable number of younger historians in the Federal Republic, for reasons that had much to do with their perception of the recent German past. This perception involved a critical confrontation with the ways in which the German historical profession had viewed and written its national history.[11] While the historians who represented the traditional approaches to German history and politics had still dominated the German universities in the 1950s, their monopoly was broken in the 1960s, as they retired and as German universities continued their process of expansion into the early 1970s.[12] In 1971 the University of Bielefeld was founded as a center in which interdisciplinary studies were given a special place, a Center for Interdisciplinary Research. Wehler was appointed to a chair of history there in 1971 and was joined in 1972 by Jürgen Kocka. Critical social history thus acquired a firm institutional basis. In 1972 the monograph series "Critical Studies in Historical Science" was launched, in which now over a hundred volumes have appeared, followed in 1975 by the journal *Geschichte und Gesellschaft* (History and Society),[13] which came to occupy a place in German scholarship not unlike that of the *Annales* in France and *Past and Present* in Great Britain.

In contrast to most of the work of the *Annales* and much of *Past and Present*, the focus of *Geschichte und Gesellschaft* and of the "Critical Studies" series was not on the medieval or early modern world but on the processes of transformation in modern industrial societies. Moreover, a major concern was the interrelation of politics and society. The new German social history was quite ready to use quantitative methods, but more cautiously than the American "New Social History" or the French "*histoire sérielle.*" The intellectual precursors of Historical Social Science in Germany were not American social scientists or French *Annales* historians but Germans: Marx as mediated through Max Weber, and Max Weber himself; the historians named above who had studied in the Weimar Republic and been forced to leave Germany after 1933—Arthur Rosenberg, a Marxist, and Hans Rosenberg and Hajo Holborn, students of Friedrich Meinecke;

Eckart Kehr, who was in the United States on a Rockefeller Fellowship when he died there at the age of thirty in March 1933; and finally the sociologist-philosophers of the Frankfurt School, particularly Max Horkheimer. These influences gave the Bielefeld historians a very different coloration from the main trends of historical and sociological studies in France or the United States and led to a much greater concentration on the ideas and values that shaped a political culture. They also predisposed the new historians to emphasize hermeneutic approaches as either supplemental or integral to their empirical analyses.

Although Wehler's theoretical statements assign culture an equal place with economics and politics in defining a society, and although he interprets culture anthropologically as a complex of symbolic interactions, he has nevertheless been accused of neglecting the cultural side of history. Critics have commented that in his social history individuals disappear within overarching structures and that culture is discussed exclusively in its institutionalized forms such as churches, schools, universities, and other formal organizations. The forms of daily life in fact receive little attention. In his *Deutsche Gesellschaftsgeschichte* Wehler deals with the condition of women largely in terms of their legal and economic status. Indeed, he devotes less space to women and everyday life than does Thomas Nipperdey, whose three volumes on German History from 1800 to 1918[14] on the one hand return to a narrative political history and on the other include extensive sections on daily life, including gender.

Jürgen Kocka emerged in the 1970s as one of the leading practitioners of the critical, theoretical approach to social history or historical social science. Already in his doctoral dissertation of 1969, he had applied theoretical models to the analysis of social change.[15] Taking the example of the giant Siemens electrical firm from its inception in 1847 to the outbreak of World War I, Kocka sought to test the applicability of Weber's ideal type of bureaucracy to the emergence of a large staff of white collar employees in the private sector. In this work, and again in his subsequent comparative study of white collar employees in Germany and America between 1890 and 1940[16] in which he examined the susceptibility of the German employees to National Socialism, Kocka attempted to go beyond objective structures and processes to the political consciousness of those who participated in them. In subsequent studies he dealt with the formation of the working class from a perspective very different from that of E. P. Thompson, whom we shall examine later. For Kocka the basic forces in the creation of a modern working class continued to be economic and structural. Working with a concept of modernization, Kocka, in his massive work on class formation in the nineteenth century (1990),[17] explained the development of the modern working classes as the result of the breakthrough of wage labor as part of a process of industrialization under capitalistic conditions. Parallel with Kocka's work, other German social historians turned their attention increasingly to the social conditions that accompanied this process of industrialization.

One must, of course, take into consideration that Wehler's works were intended as works of synthesis, as societal history (*Gesellschaftsgeschichte*), not as empirical social history. However, Wehler's conception of a critical social history gave impetus to a multitude of empirical investigations in social history centering on the process of industrialization and its consequences for social stratification among artisans, industrial workers, white collar workers, and the bourgeois classes. Interest in the consequences of industrialization in Germany was not new. It was the central theme of the Working Circle for Modern Social History, founded by Werner Conze in Heidelberg in 1957, which, still an active organization today, attracted many of the younger critical social historians and published many of their works. What these critical social historians added to the earlier investigations was greater stress on theory to explain the processes of social transformation that accompanied industrialization in the German political context.

A good deal of social history in the 1970s and 1980s in Germany as well as generally in the Western countries, and somewhat later in Eastern Europe, shifted its emphasis from economic factors to culture. The two approaches need not exclude each other. The history of the working class in Germany has proceeded through several stages since the 1950s, as it has elsewhere in Western Europe and North America. The early studies that came out of Werner Conze's Working Circle focused particularly on the role of the workers' movements as they emerged during the process of industrialization in the political culture of nineteenth- and early twentieth-century Germany, and the integration or lack of integration of these movements into a national consensus.

In the studies of the conditions of working-class life by Dieter Langewiesche,[18] Franz-Josef Brüggemeier,[19] and Klaus Tenfelde[20] the focus on politics moves into the background. These studies differ both from Thompson's culturalist approach to the working class and to more pronouncedly anthropological perspectives such as Michelle Perrot's[21] and William Sewell's[22] examinations of the symbolic and ritual aspects of working-class protest. The basic sources for Langewiesche, Brüggemeier, and Tenfelde continue to be hard empirical data, rather than literary, artistic, or folkloristic. The framework is the process of industrialization with the subsequent formation of a proletarian class. All three focus on the miners in the Ruhr valley and depict carefully the transformation of working conditions in the mines, the recruitment of a working class (mostly from among Polish migrants), the relationship between workers and employers, and social and economic conflict. In particular, Brüggemeier examines housing conditions as they affected social conditions—for example, the impact of night lodgers on the family lives of an impoverished community. Industrial diseases are carefully detailed. But the workers were not only victims; in many ways they reacted and defended themselves, repeatedly in bitter strikes, but generally in less spectacular ways such as the informal drinking clubs (*Schnapskasinos*)—often not tolerated by the police—that replaced the expensive taverns where they often were not welcome. An ethnic culture rooted in Polish ways of life and religiosity separated many of these workers from their German colleagues, not only in the workplace but also during leisure hours and thus undermined the solidarity of strike actions.

Brüggemeir deals first with conditions affecting anonymous populations, examining everyday culture within the framework of political structures, authoritarian aspects of the German Empire, and the fear of the established classes of the threat posed politically and culturally to dominant values and morals. He then turns to individual biographies of miners and tries to reconstruct what their hopes and dreams were. Sometimes it emerges that the acquisition of simple pieces of clothing and shoes confers a sense of status and prestige. Thus "honor" in Weber's sense, or "symbolic capital" in Bourdieu's, has its place in the self-definition of humble men whose sense of dignity is constantly under attack. I use the term "men" here because the world Brüggemeier describes is one in which men constitute the vast majority of the work force. The women in the background form part of the economic calculation of the employers. They provide the inexpensive housing for the night lodgers without any significant remuneration for the work involved. But the biographies give a human face to what otherwise would be impersonal, collective fates. And they provide impulses for the conduct of oral history. Thus Lutz Niethammer and his associates carried out in-depth interviews with working men and their wives who lived in the Ruhr mining region in the 1930s.[23] What matters in these interviews is not the reconstruction of what was but what people remembered. The important thing is not whether these memories are correct or not but how they reflect the ways in which these men and women experienced their pasts.

The movement from the history of the working-class movement to the social history of labor focusing on the life experiences of individuals is not unique to West German scholarship. It reflects general trends in social history not only elsewhere in the West but even in the so-called socialist countries, whose turning in this direction was slower. In the socialist East, paradoxically, labor history had tended to be elitist, written from the perspective of the organized labor movement and the social democratic or, after 1917, the Communist party. An example of this is the eight-volume history of the German labor movement published in East Berlin in 1966.[24] But even in East Germany, by the mid-1970s historians became aware of the need to turn their attention to the everyday lives of working-class people. Jürgen Kuczynski in 1981 prefaced his five-volume *Geschichte des Alltags des Deutschen Volkes 1600–1945* (History of the Everyday Life of the German People 1600–1945)[25] with a call to Marxist historians to learn from the social history of nonsocialist historians in the West. Starting from classical Marxist conceptions of class, Hartmut Zwahr published in 1978 a study of the formation of the Leipzig proletariat examining how the process of industrialization and class formation was reflected in interpersonal relations, such as family ties and friendships, and in social consciousness.[26] In a particularly interesting section, using biographical materials contained in the personal files of the workers and data from vital statistics offices, he analyzed the choice of godparents among workers. By the mid-1980s a group of East German ethnologists began in collaboration with West German and Austrian scholars to write on leisure time among Berlin workers at the turn of the century.[27]

An Austrian variant of critical historical social science is to be found in the work done by Michael Mitterauer and his co-workers after his appointment to the University of Vienna in 1971 as professor of social and economic history. Very much in the manner of the Bielefeld School, Mitterauer and his associates have sought to combine the study of social structures and social processes with that of culture and life patterns. There is a much greater concentration on the family, sexuality, and adolescence in their work than in that of their German counterparts. At the same time they make extensive use of quantitative methods and display a greater openness to English and French studies in the area of historical demography and family reconstitution. But while studies such as those by the Cambridge Group for the History of Population and Social Structure in England and by the circle of historical demographers around Louis Henry in France have dwelt heavily on premodern and preindustrial societies, the Vienna group has devoted itself much more extensively to the history of the family and to problems of puberty and sexuality in the midst of an industrializing and modernizing society. Considerable importance has been attached to oral history and to the reconstruction of individual biographies.

The development of the history of labor has parallels in the history of women. The history of women also began, in Great Britain, the United States, France, Germany, and elsewhere early in the twentieth century, as a history of the organized women's, and often specifically of the suffrage, movement. In the 1960s and 1970s a great deal of women's history dealt with the role of women in the industrializing process. Then gradually more attention was given to existential aspects of women's lives. The latter, as we shall discuss later, has required reconsideration of the concepts and methods of the social sciences.[28] An interesting attempt to combine the concepts and methods of the historical social sciences with the analysis of the life experiences of individual women is Dorothee Wierling's study published in 1987 of housemaids in German middle-class households in larger cities at the turn of the century.[29] There the profession of a maid is seen as a phenomenon of a society undergoing change toward industrialization and modernization. In this transition the maids played an important role in the formation of a "bourgeois" lifestyle; without them this style would not have been possible. At the same time the maids absorbed middle-class values and transmitted them later to the working class, into which they married. Wierling's study rests on quantitative mass data; yet, by using autobiographical material, letters, and where still possible interviews, she seeks to recapture qualitative aspects of the life situations of the maids as they experienced and remembered them. Thus it remains in the tradition of German historical social science and at the same time goes beyond it.

Chapter 7

Marxist Historical Science from Historical Materialism to Critical Anthropology

Marxist historiography and Marxist thought generally have lost a great deal of their credibility and prestige following the collapse of the Soviet Union and its Eastern European client states, which considered themselves embodiments of Marxist or Marxist-Leninist ideas. The extent to which these events were responsible for the crisis of Marxist thought must not be exaggerated, however. The official Marxist philosophy of the international Communist parties had been discredited long before the collapse. We must distinguish between this form of Marxism and Marxist thought as it developed independently of party restraints outside the Eastern bloc. While so-called Western Marxism also experienced a crisis, especially after the student revolts of the 1960s, the reasons for this crisis were different. Marxist ideas contributed to a critique of modern capitalist societies and modern culture that was taken seriously by a broad segment of opinion. But this critical Marxism too lost much of its credibility because the assumptions upon which it rested were too deeply rooted in the nineteenth century to address the concerns of the postindustrial age.

Nevertheless the contribution of Marxism to modern historical science must not be underestimated. Without Marx a good deal of the body of modern social science theory, which defined itself in opposition to Marx, along with the work of Max Weber, would not be thinkable. We cannot, of course, view Marxism as a unified movement. There are the teachings of Marx and Engels, followed by a century and a half of diverse interpretations of their writings. And as we shall see, Marx's own doctrine is full of ambivalences and ambiguities. Marx was a very dogmatic but by no means a very systematic or consistent thinker. He thus operated with two quite different conceptions of science that neither he nor his followers were able to reconcile. The one view of science was essentially positivistic, sharing many of the scientific assumptions of the period between approximately 1850 and 1890, mechanistic in their conception of reality. Two concepts were basic to this outlook: (1) that objective scientific knowledge is possible, and (2) that scientific knowledge expresses itself in general statements about the lawful behavior of phenomena. For history this meant that in order to attain the rank of a science it must discover and formulate laws of historical development. Marx here differed from other positivists such as Thomas Henry Buckle and Hippolyte Taine in seeing the primary motor of lawful historical development in social conflict rooted in economic inequality. The driving force behind history was not ideas but, as Marx stated most succinctly in the preface to *A Contribution to a Critique of Political Economy*,[1] productive forces. These forces, in the course of their development, came into conflict with the social conditions they had called forth and against which they had rebelled when these became impediments to the full unfolding of productive forces. With the inevitability of a law of nature, mankind was thus propelled from the primitive conditions of the original communism of a nomadic and hunting society through the stages of ancient, feudal, and bourgeois social formation to a Communist society in which the antagonisms inherent in all previous societies were to be overcome. It is significant that for Marx, as for most of his contemporaries, the progress of mankind was centered in the Western world, which alone was dynamic while Asia and Africa (and here Marx agreed with Hegel) were stagnant.

This view of science and of history was deeply embedded in the main currents of Western thought in the nineteenth century, differing from them markedly only in its revolutionary aims.

Marx throughout his life, however, also had a very different conception of reality and knowledge that was to play a significant role in twentieth-century Marxist thought and historiography, especially outside the Soviet Bloc. The term "dialectic," often used to refer to this alternate conception, must be used with care because it too involves an inner contradiction. On the one hand the dialectic repudiates the positivistic notion of the primacy of the phenomenal world for science, because it holds that all visible manifestations are problematic and must be understood within the broader context of conflicting forces. In Marx's young phase in 1844, as well as in the *Grundrisse* of 1857–58 and the first chapter of Volume 1 of *Das Kapital* of 1867, generally considered an expression of the mature Marx, he questions the assumption of classical political economy that the world of economics can be understood in terms of the economic forces operating in them, and he demands that they be measured in terms of human needs. Far from positing the primacy of material forces generally associated with his historical materialism, this dialectical view, notwithstanding Marx's materialistic discourse, repudiates a conception that places material forces ahead of human ones. It thus rejects political economy, or rather the economic system that operates on its premises, because it places the requirements of capital ahead of the innermost needs and aspirations of human beings. From this comes the notion of alienated labor in the 1844 manuscripts[2] and Marx's observation in *Das Kapital* that the political economy of capital belongs to "a state of society, in which the process of production has the mastery over man, instead of being controlled by him."[3] The dialectic as a philosophic method, beginning with Socrates, is a form of reasoning that proceeds by pointing out the contradictions inherent in an argument, forcing a reformulation, and going on to examine the contradictions in the new formulation. The dialectical method thus becomes the basis for a critical theory that looks at the irrationalities, in this case the violations of human dignity, contained in every social formation. But on the other hand, Marx merges his critique of positivism with an essentially positivistic conception of a law-governed process in which the dialectic takes a materialist form leading to the fulfillment of history in a communist society.

This dogmatic, essentially positivistic perception of the dialectic became the basis for the official Marxist or rather Marxist-Leninist doctrine of the established Communist parties within and outside the Soviet Bloc. Leninism introduced a new note into Marxist doctrine that was not present in Marx's writings. Marx assumed that the overall direction of the historical process was given, although the concrete forms it would take were affected by political action, thus leaving a sphere of freedom. Yet revolutions occurred only after historical development had prepared the way. In Marx's words: "No social order ever perishes before all the productive forces for which there is room in it have developed."[4] Lenin modified this notion by a voluntarism that stressed the centrality of the party. From this followed the subordination of historical research and writing to the day-by-day strategies of the party.

We must guard against a simplistic image of historical studies in the Soviet Union and the Soviet Bloc. All of the Soviet-dominated states were dictatorships that sought to exert a high degree of control over the writing and teaching of history and to utilize it for their political purposes. But there were considerable differences between the states incorporated in this system and within the individual states. The official doctrine was Marxism-Leninism, of which a central part was historical and dialectical materialism with its conception of class struggle and the displacement of one social formation by the next higher one. In all countries of the Soviet Bloc, the Central Committee of the Party and the Party Congresses set guidelines for historical studies. But within this framework there was considerable diversity.

Perhaps we can distinguish several separate areas of historical study in which ideological controls functioned differently. Dearest to the party was a historiography that was actually far removed from Marx's conception of society and history and served the political interests of the party at the moment. Particularly in the areas of contemporary history, the history of the party since 1917, and the confrontation of the Soviet Union with capitalist states, although a Marxist phraseology was used, the immediate aim was polemical and opportunistic rather than scientific: to attack forms of political deviation. On a second, macrohistorical level, the Marxist phraseology and scheme of history was imposed on larger historical processes; analysis in terms of class conflict was also mandatory in the reconstruction of specific revolutionary events or crises. Yet the farther the subject of historical research was from actual questions of present-day politics, the greater was the freedom of the historian, particularly in classical, Byzantine, and medieval history, but also, as we shall see, in social and cultural history. To be sure, quotations from Marx, Engels, and Lenin, and before 1956 also from Stalin, were required, but these were often perfunctory and not central to research based on careful examination of the archival materials. One weakness of much, but by no means all, of this research was that it often restricted itself to a relatively unreflective accumulation of facts. If the works of synthesis suffered from the imposition of grand but flawed theories, the works of archival research lacked the theoretical sophistication and consideration that give a work more than antiquarian value. Nevertheless, even in this restrictive setting, serious and imaginative work was done, though with more difficulty in the Soviet Union and in East Germany,[5] where strict control was combined with an unusual degree of docility on the part of historians. In Poland[6] after 1956, the year of Khrushchev's speech before the 20th Party Congress in the Soviet Union and of the Poznan riots in Poland, historians managed largely to free themselves from ideological guidelines. Only where their studies touched on the immediate political interests of the party or the relationship with the Soviet Union, such as the Katyn massacre, were severe restrictions imposed. Before the war there had developed a school of economic and social historians best represented by Franciszek Bujak and Jan Rutkowski, who had maintained close contact with Bloch and Febvre. Thus in 1926 a journal was founded in Poland with interests very similar to those of the *Annales d'histoire économique et sociale*, founded three years later, and with a similar title *Rocznike Dziejow Społecznych i Gospodarczych* (Annals of Social and Economic History). In 1956 this interest in economic and social history in the tradition of Bujak and Rutkowski was taken up again and the contacts with the Annales were reestablished.

There were points at which Marxist and *Annales* approaches were very compatible. Thus the work of the new Institute for the

History of Material Culture in Poland fitted in well with *Annales* interests in popular culture. Witold Kula's *Economic Theory of the Feudal System*[7] was speedily translated into French with an introduction by Fernand Braudel. Polish historians also frequently contributed to the *Annales*. Kula, in his work *Measures and Men*,[8] sought to explore the symbolic meaning of weights throughout Western history. Jerzy Topolski, in his journal *Studia Metodologiczne* and in the English-language *Poznan Studies in the Social Sciences and the Humanities*, initiated a dialogue with non-Marxist historians on questions of theory and method. In Hungary historiography moved along similar lines. In Czechoslovakia attempts to reestablish contact with international historical scholarship were seriously restricted after the Soviet military occupation of the country in 1968. But also, in the Soviet Union, important works appeared that did not fit into the narrow confines of the orthodox Marxist-Leninist philosophy and theology of history. Mikhail Bakhtin's lasting contribution in the 1930s to historical anthropology and semiotics comes to mind,[9] which, it must be noted, earned him serious persecution in the Stalin era. And, as we already mentioned, Aaron Gurevich in Moscow, in *The Categories of Medieval Culture* in 1971[10] and in subsequent works, laid the foundations in the Soviet Union for a non-Marxist history of mentalities.

But official Marxist theory, despite its rigidity and sterility, could raise questions that were productive for social history. We have already mentioned the interest historians in the Soviet Bloc showed in questions of material culture. A large-scale project in East Germany, begun in the late 1970s, undertook a comprehensive interdisciplinary study of the culture of the Magdeburg Plain during the eighteenth and early nineteenth centuries, a period of growing urbanization and of the commercialization of agriculture.[11] In their determination to proceed from an economic and social base to aspects of culture, food, fashions, architecture, festivals, etc., these studies resembled the search for the *histoire totale* of a region by *Annales* historians. The emphasis on the working population in Marxist doctrine should have stimulated studies of working-class life, but at least in the Soviet Union and in East Germany, working-class history meant the history of the organized workers movement, the Social Democrats until

1917, and the Communists thereafter. A good deal of it was political history dealing with the role of the proletariat in specific revolutionary situations. And despite proclamations to the contrary, it was generally an elitist history from above. A good example of this, already mentioned, is the eight-volume history of the German working class published by the Central Committee of the East German Socialist Unity Party in 1966, which proudly identifies its sources as the Marxist classics and "the resolutions of the party of the working class and the addresses and essays of the functionaries of the German working-class movement."[12] Jürgen Kuczynski, the doyen of East German economic historians, complained in his history of everyday life[13] that Marxist historians in East Germany had not been able to write a history of the actual everyday life experiences of the common people, and asked his colleagues to look for models in non-Marxist historiography in the West, particularly those of the *Annales*.

Thus by the time the Soviet system collapsed in 1989, a great number of historians in Eastern Europe and in the Soviet Union were aware of the inadequacies of orthodox Marxist-Leninist theory. A more serious reexamination of the Marxist tradition from a Marxist perspective in light of the changing conditions of life and thought in the twentieth century took place outside the Soviet Union, in Western Europe. It is often, of course, difficult to define what constitutes Marxism in countries where it is not an official ideology. When we speak in this section of Marxist historiography, we refer to historians who considered themselves Marxists and of whom many at one time or other, generally in the early stages of their careers, belonged to Communist parties. Thus in Great Britain there existed from 1947 until 1956 a formally organized "Communist Party's Historians Group," to which belonged several of the historians who later would attain eminence in Great Britain, such as Maurice Dobb, Rodney Hilton, Christopher Hill, Eric Hobsbawm, and Edward P. Thompson.[14] A large number of Marxist historians broke with the Communist party in 1956 at the time of the invasion of Hungary and after Krushchev's speech to the 20th Congress of the Soviet Communist Party in protest against the repressive practices of the Soviet Union. Nevertheless in many cases, such as Edward Thompson, historians who left the party continued to identify themselves with a Marxist critique of society.

In the early years after World War II Marxist discussions in the West took place largely within the framework of orthodox Marxist conceptions of the historical process. Thus Maurice Dobb and Paul Sweezy engaged in a debate on the transition from feudalism to capitalism.[15] At issue was whether, as Dobb argued, feudalism collapsed because of its own internal economic contradictions or, as Sweezy maintained, the rise of commerce constituted a decisive external factor in its demise. Parallel discussions were held among Marxist historians in France, Italy, Poland, and elsewhere. By themselves these debates should have been of interest only to a small circle of committed believers, but they aroused considerable interest outside this narrow circle. Marxist interpretations represented a challenge to non-Marxist historiography less on political grounds than because they questioned a traditional event- and person-oriented history and called for greater attention to social context and social change. What interested non-Marxist historians were less the often dogmatic answers offered by Marxists than the questions they asked. Thus the journal *Past and Present*, founded by British Marxist historians in 1952, but not controlled by the party,[16] soon became a forum for discussions between Marxist and leading non-Marxist historians such as Lawrence Stone, T. S. Ashton, John Elliott, and Geoffrey Elton. With its broad interest in society and culture, it began to occupy a place in Great Britain not unlike that of the *Annales* in France. There the great controversies about the crisis of the aristocracy and the role of class in the Puritan Revolution were carried out. Parallel discussions involving French, British, and North American historians took place in French historical studies, where the Marxist thesis of the French Revolution as a bourgeois revolution, proposed by Albert Mathiez, Albert Soboul, and in a much more complex form by Georges Lefebvre, was challenged by Alfred Cobban, George Taylor, and François Furet.

But very soon Marxist studies of the great political upheavals in modern history and of the Industrial Revolution turned their attention away from anonymous social processes to focus on the forms these changes assumed in the consciousness of those who experienced them. Marx had not succeeded in writing a history from below, but Engels had come closer to such a history in his *Condition of the Working Class in England* and his *Peasant War in Germany*. Marx's *The Eighteenth Brumaire of Louis Bonaparte* marked a step forward beyond the "Communist Manifesto" toward a differentiated examination of political change. When writing *The Eighteenth Brumaire* in 1852, Marx was forced to come to terms with the predictions he and Engels had made in January 1848 in the "Communist Manifesto," in which they had correctly foreseen that revolution was imminent but incorrectly predicted that these revolutions, which they considered to be bourgeois in character, would not only succeed but at least in Germany be followed quickly by a proletarian revolution. The course of events with which Marx dealt in *The Eighteenth Brumaire of Louis Bonaparte* in France and he and Engels in *Revolution and Counterrevolution in Germany* had shown both predictions to be wrong. To explain the failure of the revolution in France and the accession of Louis Bonaparte, Marx now proposed a picture of modern society that was much more complex than the one he and Engels had drawn in the "Communist Manifesto" and that recognized sharp social and political divisions within the bourgeoisie as well as the role played in political consciousness and behavior by noneconomic forces such as patriotic memories and symbols. Although Marx argued that political events could be understood only in the context of conflicting class interests, he created a narrative in which the members of these classes, the broad public, were left out and political personalities occupied the center of the stage very much as in conventional political histories. The workers were astonishingly absent. As for the peasants, who made up the great majority of the French population, Marx saw them as a totally passive force that, in a remarkable passage, he compared to a "sackful of potatoes."[17] And in contrast to Jules Michelet's *History of the French Revolution*, women do not appear at all. Moreover, Marx has only contempt for the really downtrodden, the homeless, the addicts, and the incarcerated, whom he lumps together as *Lumpenproletariat*,[18] lacking the discipline and the work ethic that Marx associates with the working class.

In contrast to this, English and French Marxist studies of the political and economic upheavals in medieval and modern Europe began to give history a human face. Georges Lefebvre paved the way with *The Great Fear of 1789: Rural Panic in Revolutionary France*,[19] in which he examined the panic in the countryside that had led to the peasant unprisings in the summer of 1789. Ronald Hilton did something similar for the peasant uprisings in medieval England,[20] Christopher Hill for the lower classes in the English revolutions of the seventeenth century,[21] and the African-American activist W. E. B. Du Bois for the Black population in the South during the Reconstruction after the American Civil War.[22] George Rudé[23] and Richard Cobb[24] went to the police archives to examine who concretely made up the revolutionary crowds. In his analysis of disturbances in Great Britain and France in the eighteenth and early nineteenth centuries, Rudé assigned a central role to food prices. But already in the now classic essay "The Moral Economy of the English Crowd in the Eighteenth-Century,"[25] E. P. Thompson stressed the role of noneconomic factors such as the idea of a just price that derived from traditional, precapitalistic conceptions of economic justice. The conflict between the traditional cultural values of the lower classes and the emerging capitalist economy and bureaucratic state are the theme of Eric Hobsbawm's *Primitive Rebels*[26] and his and Rudé's *Captain Swing*.[27] The similarity of these studies to those of the *Annales* is striking in their preference for the premodern world. Important exceptions are Hobsbawm's great works of synthesis, titles that span the world from the French Revolution to the collapse of communism.[28] These works focus on grand lines of development that shaped the modern world and assign a subordinate role to popular culture.

Perhaps the most important single work of history in this movement to a Marxist history that stressed the role of popular culture was Edward P. Thompson's *The Making of the English Working Class* (1963). The title proclaims Thompson's thesis that "the working class did not rise like the sun at an appointed time. It was present at its own making."[29] In this book and in his later theoretical statements, he took issue with Marxist orthodoxy and its defense by structuralists such as the French philosophers, specifically Louis Althusser, who stressed the scientific aspects of

Marxism.[30] For Thompson the writings of Marx are not decisive for Marxist opinion in the mid-twentieth century. He thus distinguishes "between Marxism as closure and a tradition, derivative from Marx, of open investigation and critique. The first stands in the tradition of theology. The second is a tradition of active reason" that has liberated itself from "the truly scholastic notion that the problems of our time (and the experiences of our century) will become understood by the rigorous scrutiny of a text published one hundred and twenty years ago."[31] From Marx, Thompson adopts the concept of class and the notion that "the class experience is largely determined by the productive relations into which men are born—or enter involuntarily."[32] But class must be seen not as "a 'structure,' nor even 'category,' but as something which in fact happens (and can be shown to have happened) in human relationships."[33] "Class consciousness [is that consciousness] in which these experiences are handled in cultural terms: embodied in traditions, value-systems, ideas, and institutional forms."[34] Thus Thompson rejects the idea of a "prototypical" working class and instead turns to "a concrete English working class," which emerged within a specific historical context. The stress on culture signifies a turn away from scientific methods, which objectify human relations, toward approaches that yield understanding of the qualitative elements that make up a culture; hence his reliance on literature, art, folklore, symbolism.

Thompson here rejects three basic Marxist concepts: the primacy of economic forces, the objectivity of scientific method, and the idea of progress. He resists the idea that the past is a step to the future. He thus is "seeking to rescue the poor stockinger, the Luddite cropper, the 'obsolete' hand-loom weaver, the 'utopian' artisan, and even the deluded follower of Joanna Southcott from the enormous condescension of posterity," although "their hostility to the new industrialism may have been backward-looking."[35]

Nevertheless important elements of orthodox Marxism survive in Thompson's approach. In his study, confined admittedly to England, he defends the notion that there is one working class against the idea of a much more diverse working population marked by different ethnic, religious, and craft traditions. Bestowing a halo on this class, he sees it very much as Marx does, as an aristocracy of labor. Important thinkers such as Paine,

Cobbett, and Owen, The London Corresponding Society, and the political traditions of English radicalism thus play a crucial role in the formation of the working class. In this respect *The Making of the English Working Class* is more a history of ideas than of experiences. Class conflict occupies center stage in the book. And despite its cultural components, this conflict is rooted in the economic system.[36] Were it not, the link to Marxism would be tenuous. But it has led critics to note justly that other forms of conflict and exploitation, including those involved in gender relations, are neglected.[37]

Among Marxists, Thompson's approach to history came under critical scrutiny from two diverse directions. It was criticized on the one hand, from the perspective of the structuralist Marxism of the French philosopher Louis Althusser, as a form of "socialist humanism" that "suppresses Marx's major substantive achievements—the analysis of the forms, tendencies and laws of the capitalist modes of production."[38] On the other hand cultural Marxists argued that Thompson had not yet emancipated himself sufficiently from orthodox assumptions that overstressed the objective aspects of economic relations.[39] Even if he saw class in terms of culture, they charged, this culture still focused on an industrial working class in which those not directly linked to the industrial work process had little role. Despite Thompson's concern to rescue Joanna Southcott from the "enormous condescension of posterity," the same could be said for his general neglect of women, who after all were not direct parts of the productive process as it had been commonly understood by socialists and nonsocialists alike.

History Workshop, founded, as the subtitle indicated, as "a journal of socialist historians," built on Thompson's approach to labor history but went beyond it. The transformation of the journal from its founding in 1976 until 1995, when it dropped its subtitle (modified in 1982 to "a journal of socialist and feminist historians"), documented fundamental changes that took place in Marxist approaches to history in Great Britain and elsewhere. The term "workshop" was intentionally chosen both to denote the Marxist concern with work and the workshop and to create a history written jointly with historians who come from the workplace. It placed itself within a tradition of socialist and radical scholarship that in Great Britain went back to the Hammonds and the Webbs, included the writers of the Communist Party Historians' Group, and received an "enormous impetus" from E. P. Thompson. It acknowledged *Past and Present*, founded in 1952 by a group of historians "with a distinctly left-wing political outlook," as "the best historical journal in the English language"[40] and set out to supplement its work and also to give it a new direction.

But what distinguished *History Workshop* from other historical journals was not its socialist commitment—shared by many of the original contributors of *Past and Present* as well, half of whose original editorial board had been members of the Communist party—but its proclaimed intention to break out of the narrow confines of professional history in order "to reach and serve a wide democratic audience rather than a closed circle of academic peers."[41] In the long run it achieved this aim only very incompletely. The opening editorial of the first issue began with a tirade against the professionalization of historical studies that had led to their "increasing fragmentation,"[42] their political and social irrelevance, their loss of autonomy, and the sclerosis of an academia embedded in a capitalist society. The journal itself was the outcome of ten years of close cooperation among men and women historians gathered together in a "workshop" at Ruskins College, the labor college at Oxford University. It is important both that the editorial board was viewed as a collective that in fact made collective decisions, although Gareth Stedman Jones, Raphael Samuel, and Tim Mason, all of whom had already made important contributions to academic social history, stood out, and that women were well represented among the editors as well as the contributors. The editorials in the first issue already contained a commitment to "feminist history." They pointed out that not only established political history but also labor and social history had confined themselves within an "anti-feminist definition," because women, although their labor as "the reproducers of labor power" constituted an integral part of the work process in a capitalist economy,[43] remained largely invisible in these histories by virtue of their invisibility in the public workplace.

This focus on the role of women contributed to a broadening in the scope of the journal as well as to an exploration of new methodological approaches. To begin with, *History Workshop* was committed to its conception of "socialist history," which was closely linked to "labour history" in an industrial capitalist society. Despite their reorientation of Marxist history toward culture, the editors were committed in ways very similar to Thompson's to orthodox Marxist notions of the historical process. They clung to a teleology that saw history as transforming by stages from feudalism, to capitalism, to the overcoming of capitalism in a socialist society. Hence it is indicative that the very first article of the journal was Ronald Hilton's "Feudalism and the Origins of Capitalism."[44] Modern society was characterized for the journal by industrial production under capitalist traditions in the presence of a class-conscious working class. Attention was given to the ways in which workers experienced labor under these conditions, but the workers were almost all industrial workers in nineteenth- and early twentieth-century Great Britain. The experiences of women were also placed in this context. Very soon, however, Raphael Samuel, one of the editors, began to question the identity of industrialism and capitalism and to recognize both the large role played by non-mechanical labor and traditional crafts in the capitalist economy of the nineteenth century and the role played by capitalism in nonindustrial sectors of the economy, principally agriculture.[45]

In "10 Years After" (1985)[46] the editors of *History Workshop*, in an editorial signed by Raphael Samuel and Gareth Stedman Jones, recognized errors in judgment. "The unspoken centre of our interest was the industrial working class, and the summit of our ambition (as it appeared in the original manifesto) was the study of capitalism as a 'mode of production.'" "Feminism," they added, "has put this teleology into question." The teleology had further become problematic as a result of the structural changes in capitalism that had become increasingly apparent during the decade preceding 1985—changes that had revealed class relations to be different and much more complex than previously supposed. In fact the treatment of women in the journal had shifted since the early issues from the industrial workplace to the domestic and the private sphere and was increasingly concerned with sexuality. The exploitation of women was seen in the broader context of gender relations. Differences in leisure activities—or the lack of such for women—were examined as well as the role of violence in defining male identity.

Beginning in 1980, the journal devoted increasing space to the role of language as a constituent factor in social experience. Rejecting the radical position of structural linguistics represented by Lacan, Foucault, and Derrida, for whom "there is no external reality to which language refers; hence no dialectical tension and no principle of change," the editors nevertheless emphasized that "the language of socialism . . . antedates the appearance of a socialist movement"[47] and has in fact contributed substantially to the formation of that movement. But "far from existing in its own syntactically structured realm," as the structural linguists have insisted, language, as Pierre Achard argued in "History and the Politics of Language in France,"[48] "has been a more or less continuous site of political and ideological struggle." Looking at language from a broad anthropological perspective, Maurice Godelier maintained "that its meanings have never been vested exclusively in language systems or texts, but have been conditioned by changes in the labour process, in kin systems, in status hierarchies, and in the whole ensemble of the symbolic and material forms of a society."[49] Further, the journal agrees with feminist theorists that gender is not a natural given but a cultural construct embedded in language, while at the same time seeing language itself as reflecting as well as acting upon society. Until the 1990s, the focus was very much on industrial Europe and North America. The non-Western world appeared in the earlier issues largely in the shadow of an expanding imperialism; now, in essays in the 1990s, Latin America, Africa, and aboriginal Australia receive a greater degree of individual attention.

Thatcherism and, despite their rejection of Leninism, the collapse of the Soviet Union and the Eastern European socialist systems deeply shook the Marxist convictions of *History Workshop*'s editors. Already in 1985, they admitted that "the existence of a labour movement as one of the geological certainties of the landscape," which had been one of the basic assumptions of the journal at its founding, "can no longer be taken for granted." Painfully they recognized "the severance of the socialist ideas from any notion of popular will."[50] Quietly in the spring of 1995 they dropped the subtitle "a journal of socialist and feminist historians." They noted that "the political conditions in which we work have changed almost out of recognition in the fourteen years since [in 1981] we last amended our mast-head" to include "feminist historians." The conditions under which radical historians could identify themselves as Marxists no longer prevailed. The challenges of the contemporary world—environmental, ethnic, sexual—had become so complex that the terms "socialist" and "feminist" with the connotations they had carried no longer sufficed.[51]

The journal had succeeded in its aim to span disciplinary boundaries, but this had been true of other important journals too, most noteworthy the *Annales, Past and Present, Quaderni Storici*, and the *Journal of Interdisciplinary History*. It had not been very successful in bridging the gap between professional historians and nonacademics. By the mid-1990s its contributors were overwhelmingly attached to universities or research institutions. We may ask, what remains of the original faith and purpose of the journal? Not only the Marxist teleology but also the conception of class that was fundamental to its understanding of society and of political practice was irredeemably shaken. Nevertheless the commitment to a history that was close and understandable to the common woman and man remained. Paradoxically, as the journal freed itself of its Marxist assumptions, it was able to come closer to the experiences of common people than it had been from a Marxist understanding of work and working people. Finally, the journal has maintained the critical stance of Marxism, the dedication to confronting all forms of exploitation and domination embedded in the society. But unlike orthodox Marxism it no longer finds these primarily in the institutional framework of the economy and the state, but seeks them in all aspects of life, including the relation of the sexes.

The place of *History Workshop* in the historiography of the past two decades should not be overstated. It was one of a number of journals internationally that took a similar direction. It recognized its debt to *Past and Present* but from the beginning went further in the direction of popular history and culture and attempted, even if with limited success, to recruit common people. As a movement it was imitated elsewhere, particularly in the Federal Republic of Germany and in Sweden. Similar concerns were reflected in a variety of journals: *Social History* in Great Britain; the *Journal of Social History* and the *Radical History Review* in the United States; and *Quaderni Storici* in Italy, which moved away from a focus on institutions to one that placed the existential experiences of a broad section of the population into the center of historical interest. *Historische Anthropologie*, founded in 1993 in Germany and Austria, and *Odysseus*, established in Moscow in 1991, are the most recent journals to join these efforts.

III

History and the Challenge of Postmodernism

Chapter 8

Lawrence Stone and "The Revival of Narrative"

In 1979 there appeared in *Past and Present*, which had been since its founding in 1952 the most important forum in Great Britain for discussions in history and the social sciences, Lawrence Stone's essay "The Revival of Narrative: Reflections on a New Old History."[1] In this now famous piece, Stone notes that in the 1970s a basic transformation took place in the way history was viewed and written. The belief central to social science history, that "a coherent scientific explanation of change in the past"[2] is possible, was widely rejected. In its place there emerged a renewed interest in the most varied aspects of human existence, accompanied by the conviction "that the culture of the group, and even the will of the individual, are potentially at least as important causal agents of change as the impersonal forces of material output and demographic growth."[3] This renewed emphasis on the experiences of concrete human beings ushered in a return to narrative forms of history.

The turn to experience involved a critical reexamination of scientific rationality. Social science-oriented history had presupposed a positive relationship to a modern, expanding industrial world in which science and technology contributed to growth and development. But this faith in progress and in the civilization of the modern world has undergone a serious test since the 1960s. In the 1950s American historians and social scientists still spoke complacently of a national "consensus" and of a truly classless society, free from deeper social conflicts, which distinguished America, past and present, from Europe. John Kenneth Galbraith in 1958 published *The Affluent Society*.[4] As we already mentioned, Daniel Bell's *The End of Ideology* appeared in 1960,[5] followed in 1962 by Michael Harrington's *The Other America*,[6] which focused on those segments of the American population, the poor, White and Black, who had been excluded from the affluence and did not share in the consensus. In the United States the previously hidden tensions in the society came to the fore in full force with the civil disobedience movement of the early 1960s and the bloody uprisings in the ghettos in the second half of that decade. The Vietnam War then divided Americans as profoundly as the Algerian War had divided the French a few years earlier. But the opposition to the war went beyond purely political issues. The conflicts of the second half of the 1960s, triggered in the United States by the conflicts about civil rights and about the Vietnam War, focused not only on criticism of existing political and social conditions, but also on the quality of life in a highly industrialized society. The faith in progress and science, which was basic not only to the quantitative New Economic history but also to Marxism, became increasingly problematic in view of the dangers and the brutality with which technology transformed the industrial countries and affected the developing nations.

It is important to realize that the student movement of the late 1960s in Berkeley, Paris, Berlin, and Prague turned against both capitalism in the West and the Soviet form of Marxism. This is important for the developments within historiography if one is to understand why neither the usual social-scientific models nor historical materialism could continue to be convincing. Both start from macrohistorical and macrosocietal conceptions for which the state, the market, or for Marxism the class, are central concepts. In both, the firm belief in the possibility and desirability of scientifically steered growth is taken for granted. The focus on social structures and social processes, shared by orthodox social science and orthodox Marxism, left little room for those segments of the population who had previously been neglected and who now claimed an identity and a history of their own. Moreover, both social science and Marxist historiography

showed little interest in the existential aspects of everyday life—
its material, but also its emotional side, its hopes and fears.

A pessimistic view regarding the course and quality of modern Western civilization occupied a central place in much of the
"New Cultural History." This new history maintained a paradoxical relationship to Marxism. It shared the Marxist view regarding the emancipatory function of historiography; but it
understood the constraints from which men and women were to
be emancipated quite differently from classical Marxists. The
sources of exploitation and domination were not to be found
primarily in institutionalized structures, in politics or in the
eonomy, but more importantly in the many interpersonal relations in which human beings exert power over others. Gender
thus also assumed a new and significant role. Foucault in an
important sense replaced Marx as the analyst of power and of its
relation to knowledge.

One key question raised by Stone was whether and in what
way history could or should understand itself as a science. Not
only social science-oriented historiography, but also the older
tradition of critical historical research as it had developed with
Ranke in the nineteenth-century universities viewed history as a
science. However, for the latter science had had a different
meaning. It involved the repudiation of the positivism of the
analytical social sciences and emphasized the distinction between the human or cultural sciences (*Geisteswissenschaften*)
and the natural sciences. It nevertheless adhered to a concept of
science and viewed history as a scientific discipline. Hence in
Germany the term *Geschichtswissenschaft* (historical science)
replaced the term *Geschichtsschreibung* (the writing of history)
to describe what professional historians were doing. The concept
science here involved the centrality of a logic of inquiry that set
rigorous methodological guidelines for obtaining objective
knowledge. While stressing the role of empathy in historical
understanding, which involved the subjectivity of the historian,
this school of historical scholarship nevertheless had posited a
clear line of distinction between historical scholarship and imaginative literature. It should, however, be stressed that this distinction between analysis and narration was frequently not adhered
to. Georges Duby in *The Legend of Bouvines*[7] and Jacques Le

Goff in his recent biography of Saint Louis,[8] as we shall see later, demonstrated that narration occupied an important place in the *Annales* tradition.

Although Stone emphatically rejected the illusion of "coherent scientific explanation" in history, he nowhere suggested that historical narrative, despite its necessarily literary form, surrenders its claim to rational inquiry and realistic reconstruction. But as we saw in the introduction, a number of theorists in France and the United States, mostly coming from literary criticism, such as Roland Barthes, Paul De Man, Hayden White, Jacques Derrida, and Jean-François Lyotard,[9] frequently identified as postmodernists—a label some of them would vigorously reject—would call for this surrender and question the distinction between fact and fiction, history and poetry. They viewed history as having no reference to a reality outside of its texts. But as we shall see, practicing historians seldom went so far. There was no radical break between the older social science history and the new cultural history, but the themes and with them the methods of the new historiography changed as the center of gravity shifted from structures and processes to cultures and the existential life experiences of common people. While this involved a greater skepticism regarding the claims of the traditional social sciences, it did not mean a flight into the imaginary. Not only did historians continue to work conscientiously and critically with sources, but, as we shall see in the following sections, they also adopted methods and findings from the social sciences. Thus they by no means gave up the conviction that the historian must follow rational methods to gain truthful insights into the past.

Chapter 9

From Macro- to Microhistory: The History of Everyday Life

Increasingly in the 1970s and 1980s historians not only in the West, but in some cases also in the Eastern European countries, began to question the assumptions of social science history. The key to the worldview of social science history, as seen by its critics, was the belief in modernization as a positive force. In its most radical form this belief was voiced in Francis Fukuyama's 1989 essay "The End of History,"[1] which proclaimed that a modern technological society based on capitalist free market principles accompanied by representative parliamentary institutions signified the achievement of a rational order of things as the outcome of historical development. A good deal less sanguine, other social science-oriented historians such as Jürgen Kocka, aware of the destructive aspects of modern societies, nevertheless expressed their confidence in the overall positive character of modernization, whereby a market economy and a highly developed technology would be coupled with democratic political institutions guaranteeing civil liberties, social justice, and cultural pluralism.[2] For Kocka the collapse both of Nazism and of the Marxist-Leninist systems in Eastern Europe and the Soviet Union seemed to confirm this point. A key function of a critical historical social science was, in his view, to point at the atavistic aspects of social orders in the twentieth century that stood in the way of a truly modern society, as Wehler and he had done in their analysis of German society before 1945.

For Carlo Ginzburg and Carlo Poni, two of the most important representatives of microhistory in Italy, the key reason for the decline of macrohistorical conceptions and with them of social science approaches to history was to be found in the loss of faith in just this optimistic view of the beneficial social and political fruits of technological progress.[3] The arguments made against macrohistorical social science approaches, which included Marxism, were based on political and ethical grounds even more than on methodological ones, although, as we shall see, the Italian school in particular subjected the basic assumptions of social science history to a searching methodological critique. A key objection to the social science conception of a world historical process characterized by modernization was, in their view, the human cost. This process, they argued, has unleashed not only immense productive forces but also devastating destructive energies that are inseparably linked with them. Moreover, it has taken place, so to say, behind the backs of people, primarily "little people," who had been neglected as much in social science-oriented history as they had been in the conventional political history that focused on the high and mighty. History must turn to the conditions of everyday life as they are experienced by common people. But the kind of history of everyday life that Fernand Braudel had offered in the 1960s and 1970s in *The Structures of Everyday Life*[4] for them missed the point by attending to material conditions without examining how these conditions were experienced.

We have already pointed to the role that political beliefs played not only in the scholarship of the older school of political historiography but also in more recent forms of social history and, of course, in Marxism. They play the same role, and perhaps a more readily apparent one in the new microhistorical studies of everyday life. It is not coincidental that in Italy many historians, like many of their British colleagues, began as professed Marxists and then moved in directions that challenged the basic macrohistorical conceptions of Marxism. The subject matter of historical studies moved, for the historians of everyday life, from what they call the "center" of power to the "margins," to the many, and the many are for them overwhelmingly the disadvantaged and the exploited. This stress on disadvantage and exploitation distinguishes this historiography from older romantic traditions of the history of popular life such as the nineteenth-century ethnology of Wilhelm Riehl.[5] While Riehl looked nostalgically back to an idyllic folk society free of inner conflicts, the historians of everyday life emphasize the lack of harmony.

The many, however, are not viewed by these historians as part of a crowd but as individuals who must not be lost either within world historical processes or in anonymous crowds. Edward Thompson had already made clear the motivation of his history when he proclaimed the aim of *The Making of the English Working Class* to be "to rescue the poor stockinger . . . [and] the 'obsolete' hand-loom weaver . . . from the enormous condescension of posterity."[6] But if one wishes to rescue the unknown from oblivion, a new conceptual and methodological approach to history is called for that sees history no longer as a unified process, a grand narrative in which the many individuals are submerged, but as a multifaceted flow with many individual centers. Not history but histories, or, better, stories, are what matter now. And if we are dealing with the individual lives of the many, we need an epistemology geared to the experiences of these many that permits knowledge of the concrete rather than the abstract.

By the 1970s a history that anchored culture in a firm political, social, and economic context had been prepared in the great works of George Duby on marriage, the perpetuation of national myths, and the social structure of feudalism[7] and in Jacques Le Goff's works on intellectuals and clerics and conceptions and patterns of work.[8] Le Goff and Duby also succeeded in writing a social and cultural history in which narrative and individuals played a central role, as in Duby's work on the Battle of Bouvines on Sunday, July 27, 1214, as a historical event that was transformed into a national myth (1973),[9] and most recently in Jacques Le Goff's 1996 biography of St. Louis.[10] In the course of the 1970s studies of popular culture became more frequent in the English-speaking and the Italian world, as in Keith Thomas's *Religion and the Decline of Magic: Studies in Popular Beliefs in 16th and 17th Century Europe* (1971),[11] Peter Burke's *Popular Culture in Early Modern Europe* (1978),[12] Natalie Z. Davis's *Society and Culture in Early Modern France* (1975),[13] and Carlo

Ginzburg's *The Cheese and the Worms: The Cosmos of a Six-teenth-Century Miller* (1975),[14] in all of which religion occupies an important place, in Davis's case with a strong focus on gender. There is no reason why a history dealing with broad social transformations and one centering on individual existences cannot cooexist and supplement each other. It should be the task of the historian to explore the connections between these two levels of historical experience. Nevertheless a vigorous debate took place in the 1980s in Germany between advocates of a social science history, who called for strict conceptual and analytical guidelines, and the champions of everyday history, for whom these guidelines meant the death knell for lived experiences, which they ardently believed should be the true subject matter of history.[15] In a crucial article, "Missionaries in the Row Boat"(1984)[16] Hans Medick sought to stake out the basic positions of everyday history. For this history, cultural anthropology as it was represented in the seventies and eighties by Clifford Geertz served as a model for historical research. This semiotic approach is pursued in Geertz's conception of a "thick description,"[17] which means an immediate confrontation with an other. It also means that we do not wish to read our preconceptions into the other but to recapture it as it is. Nevertheless, at this point Geertz and Medick become enmeshed in a seeming contradiction because the thick description they call for does not give us access to an individual but only to the culture in which he or she is bound up. Thus the "poor stockinger," whose individual dignity Thompson set out to rescue from the impersonal forces of history, now again loses his individuality to a culture since we are able to gain insight into the individual only through the culture that shapes him or her. Neither the ethnologist nor the historian, according to Geertz and Medick, has immediate access to the experience of others. Therefore he has to continue to decipher these experiences indirectly through symbolic and ritualistic acts that, proceeding beneath the immediacy of individual intentions and actions, form a text that makes access to another culture possible.

Kocka criticized Medick's approach, which he described as a "neohistoricism" (not to be confused with the New Historicism in the United States discussed earlier) on two grounds: Like the older historicism, its emphatic renunciation of theory and its insistence on immediate experience, in his opinion, led to a methodological irrationalism. One cannot have coherent insight into reality if one does not proceed with explicit questions that help us to locate what we are looking for in the immense multitude of experiences. For Medick the very approach to our subject matter with carefully formulated questions prejudices our findings; for Kocka the absence of these questions makes meaningful knowledge impossible. Moreover for Kocka the concentration on the "small" aspects of history isolated from broader contexts renders historical knowledge impossible and leads to the trivialization of history. There is therefore a danger that the history of everyday life may deteriorate into anecdotes and antiquarianism.

Now for Medick "small is beautiful" by no means signifies an anecdotal history cut loose from larger contexts. In fact, Medick insists that history should move from concern with "central" institutions to the margins, where individuals who do not conform to the established norms are to be found.[18] Nevertheless the individual can only be understood as part of a larger cultural whole. Thus the microhistory he pursues cannot stand without a macrosocial context. Not only the *Alltagsgeschichte* (everyday history) that Medick represents in Germany, but also microhistory as conceived by its Italian advocates, to whom we shall come below, assumes the existence of a comprehensive popular culture. Hence the turn to historical anthropology with its semiotic approach to the symbolic expressions of culture. For the Italians this is a peasant culture that has endured since primordial times.

At this point the protoindustrialization project launched in the early 1970s at the Max Planck Institute for History should be mentioned. The focus here was on a small unit, the peasant household. Franklin Mendels, a Belgian American who coined the term "protoindustrialism" in 1972,[19] focused on the interplay of economic forces and regenerative practices in these households. According to him cottage industries in a period of increasing demand for textiles led to an early form of industrialization and furthered the increase of population, with earlier marriages and more children, to meet the need for labor. Important studies along these lines were carried out in Great Britain and elsewhere in the early 1970s[20] and helped inspire the German project, resulting in 1979 in a collaborative volume, *Industrialization Before Industrialization*,[21] concentrating on the development of domestic industry in the countryside prior to the Industrial Revolution. Despite the reservations these historians expressed in regard to the systematic social sciences, which in their view left too little space for human initiative, they relied heavily in their work on the hard social sciences, primarily economics and historical demography. They operated with concepts of social differentiation and of a market economy that derive from classical political economy. In this sense they worked within a conceptual structure similar to the one we already noted in Emmanuel Le Roy Ladurie's analysis of the interplay of food prices and population pressures. Nevertheless with the stress on the family as the key unit in the productive process, new foci enter. From the hard framework of a quantitative demography, we move into the much more concrete setting of families in which protoindustrialization brings about changed reproductive patterns involving early marriages and childbearing as property relations change. Work patterns too change. The studies show to what extent spending, saving, and work are determined not only by economic pressures but by questions of status and honor expressed through conspicuous consumption.[22] Thus to understand the nature of a rural protoindustrial community we need to go beyond economic and demographic analysis to the consideration of culture.

In the 1980s the main participants in the protoindustrialization project at the Max Planck Institute for History, Hans Medick and Jürgen Schlumbohm, joined by an American, David Sabean (who at the time was at the Institute) proceeded from their more general studies of protoindustrialization to an examination of the process in a specific locality, Medick[23] and Sabean[24] in two villages in Suabia, Laichingen and Neckarhausen, Schlumbohm[25] in the parish of Belms in Westphalia. On one level this is a continuation of older forms of social science research. A tremendous number of data is fed into the computer, particularly concerning property inventories at marriage and death as well as vital statistics, trial records, literacy, etc. The result is a host of information that relates to culture. Inventories, for example, yield information on book possession. The focus is on one village or locality over a period of approximately two hundred years, from the old regime to the latter part of the nineteenth century. Despite the frequent tribute they pay to Geertz, their approach is very different. Instead of thick description, they work with hard material and societal data, which they then interpret. The Geertzian conception of a culture as an integrated semiotic system—not entirely different from the romantic notion of a village community that we find in nineteenth-century ethnologists like Wilhelm Riehl, nostalgic for a simpler and more harmonious folk culture—is replaced by one that sees differentiation and conflict. Moreover, the history of the localities takes place within the context of the great political, economic, and social changes in the transition from a premodern to a modern society. Although they dislike the concept of modernization, these historians work with it, in awareness of the "costs." They are thus much closer to traditional social science history and much further removed from historical anthropology than they concede.

There are great similarities and yet fundamental differences between the anthropological and microhistorical historians in Germany whom we have just discussed and the Italian practitioners of *microstoria*. Despite similarities in their political outlook, they come from two different traditions. The main representatives of the Italian tradition, Carlo Ginzburg, Carlo Poni, Giovanni Levi, and Edoardo Grendi, began as Marxists.[26] They reacted against Marxist doctrines on two grounds: One was their rejection of the authoritarian aspects of the established Communist parties. The second, which they reiterated repeatedly, was their loss of faith in the macrohistorical conceptions that Marxism shares with non-Marxist conceptions of growth. They wished to give history again a human face, which led them to react not only against traditional Marxism but also against the analytical social sciences and the *Annales*. The latter avoid the narrowness of the two former, but Braudel's house of history, as Levi notes, has many rooms permitting a variety of outlooks and approaches—but there are no people living in.[27]

The practitioners of *microstoria*, like their German colleagues, want to return to the life experiences of concrete human beings. They preserve three elements of the Marxist historical orientation, two of which they share with the Germans: The first is the belief that social inequality is a central characteristic of all historical societies. The second is the role production and reproduction play in the formation of cultures. Economic forces, they insist, do not offer an explanation for social and cultural aspects of life, but they enter into them. They constitute significant causes of social inequality without which history cannot be understood, although inequality takes on forms that extend far beyond political, economic, and social inequality as it has been traditionally conceived, particularly in the Marxist tradition. The third is the belief that historical study must be based on rigorous method and empirical analysis. While critical of traditional Marxist and social science approaches, they avoid the belief, voiced by Geertz and taken very seriously by Medick in his essay on the missionaries, that history gains many of its insights from poetry, a position voiced also, as we have seen, by Hayden White and adopted by American cultural historians like Natalie Davis[28] for whom, at least in their methodological statements, the borderline between fact and fiction becomes fluid. For the practitioners of *microstoria*, the line is much less fluid. They insist that the historian deals with a real subject matter. Their criticism of traditional social science approaches is not that social science is not possible or desirable but that social scientists have made generalizations that do not hold up when tested against the concrete reality of the small-scale life they claim to explain. There is nevertheless a certain contradiction between theory and practice in the writings of both the German and the Italian orientation. While the Italians remain skeptical of what they consider to be Geertz's methodological irrationalism, they too, particularly Carlo Ginzburg, move in their historical narratives to a position close to Geertz's thick description. Conversely, the Germans worked from the start closely with social science methods involving computer analyses of long series.

Unlike the German microhistorians, the Italians have had a firm institutional basis in the journal *Quaderni Storici*, which since its founding in 1966 had occupied a place in Italy not dissimilar to the *Annales* in France or *Past and Present* in Great Britain as a forum for a broad spectrum of historical approaches.

In Germany *Geschichte und Gesellschaft* played such a role, but with a much stronger social science orientation. Only with the founding of *Historische Anthropologie* in 1993 did a German journal come into existence representing the viewpoint of micro-history and historical anthropology.

Significantly the new journal published in its first volume an article by Carlo Ginzburg on the Italian tradition of *microstoria*.[29] The article essentially restated ideas that Ginzburg and Poni had first put forward in *Quaderni Storici* in 1979 and in other programmatic statements elsewhere. They pointed to the crisis of macrohistory as part of an increasing disillusionment in the 1970s with grand narratives. Large-scale social scientific studies based on massive quantitative computerized data were questioned, not because a social scientific approach was inapplicable but because the large-scale generalizations distorted the actual reality at the base. A basic commitment of *microstoria*, according to its practitioners, is "to open history to peoples who would be left out by other methods" and "to elucidate historical causation on the level of small groups where most of life takes place."[30]

There are affinities between the theoretical and methodological positions articulated by the advocates of *microstoria* and those of Foucault and Geertz, but also marked differences. Like Foucault they seek to show how "hegemonic institutions have excluded certain ways of thinking as demonic, irrational, heretical, or criminal,"[31] as Ginzburg did in the case of his miller philosopher and cosmologist Menocchio[32] and Levi did in the case of the parish priest Giovan Battista Chiesa.[33] And like Geertz their aim is an "interpretive" study of culture that needs to be approached "through single, seemingly insignificant, signs, rather than through the applications of laws derived from repeatable and quantifiable observations."[34] In Levi's words: "The microhistorical approach addresses the problem of how we gain access to knowledge of the past by means of various clues, signs and symptoms."[35] Yet they continue to insist that there is a reality external to the historical texts that can be known. Admittedly knowledge is mediated. Because it is, microhistorical method "breaks with the traditional assertive, authoritative form of discourse adopted by historians who present reality as objective."[36] Going back to a form of presentation that preceded that of professionalized historiography, *microstoria* introduces a narrative in which the historian transmits his/her findings but also his/her procedure. "In microhistory . . . the researcher's point of view becomes an intrinsic part of the account."[37] The narrative becomes important for the presentation of the historian's findings because it can communicate elements that cannot be conveyed in abstract form and because it shows the process by which the historian arrives at his/her account.

Yet despite these limitations placed on objectivity, *microstoria* shares several basic assumptions with older social science that serve to distinguish it from Foucault's and Geertz's approaches. For Foucault, Edward Muir notes, "theories cannot be verified because standards of verification come from a modern scientific discipline that makes the past conform to the present. Correctness means conformity to an order of things that has been defined by a discipline or an institution."[38] For Ginzburg and Levi this is "an evasion. Correctness must be determined by the concrete, physically real evidence the past presents us."[39] *Microstoria* does not reject the empirical social sciences in toto, but stresses the methodological need of testing their constructs against existing reality on a small scale. It questions Geertz's approach to culture on similar grounds. Despite Geertz's claim that he deals with a world on a small scale, he adheres to a macrosocial conception of a culture as an integrated system, a whole. As Levi notes: "It seems to me that one of the main differences in perspective between microhistory and interpretive anthropology is that the latter sees a homogenous meaning in public signs and symbols whereas microhistory seeks to define and measure them with reference to the multiplicity of social representations they produce."[40] The result is a society marked by "social differentiation."[41] Here considerations of hegemony and social inequality, which were prime concerns of Marxist historiography, shape the historical conception of the microhistorians.

We shall briefly examine two of the most representative works of the *microstoria* tradition, Carlo Ginzburg's *The Cheese and the Worms: The Cosmos of a Sixteenth-Century Miller* (1975), and Giovanni Levi, *Inheriting Power: The Story of an Exorcist*

(1985). These books have much in common and yet are very different in their conceptual and narrative approaches. Ginzburg's book has become a classic, perhaps also because it reads so well and confronts us with a very rich individual. Levi's exorcist is much more deeply embedded in social structures and the text is more analytical. Both books share the general characteristics of *microstoria*, the concentration on an individual in a given locality and the attempt to stress the difference of this very local setting from a larger norm. In both there is a careful reconstruction of the social and political setting, with the focus again on the local rather than on a broader transregional level. And yet Ginzburg's approach to his protagonist, Menocchio, is much more hermeneutic than Levi's. The primary focus is on Menocchio's mental world. And the way into his mind is through the texts he reads. Reading is not an impersonal process by which meanings are communicated; rather the writings of elite minds enter into the mind of the peasant miller through the prism of a popular culture. In turn Ginzburg's own imagination is vital in the reconstruction of Menocchio's thought processes. The narrative is interrupted by the presentation of the investigative strategies of the author. Levi's concern is much more social scientific, to test or correct established hypotheses. There are frequent passages spelling out hypotheses to be confirmed. A central concern is the pattern of power relationships in the village. These cannot be understood in terms of economic factors or formal political institutions. Levi questions the extent to which impersonal forces of the market and the development of a modern state machinery determined these power relationships. He argues that the decisive element in the understanding of the peasant world was "the preservation or transmission of intangible or symbolic goods: power and prestige."[42] To establish his point, he resorts to the sources and methods used by more traditional social history, a prosopography that relies on parish registers, notarial acts, data from land-tax surveys, and other administrative documents to reconstruct the lives of the persons exorcised by Chiesa and their social setting. He also relates data on land sales to data on the constitution of families and inheritance to demonstrate that in the place of the blind market of classical economics there operated in the village a complex market in which social and personal relationships, involving family strategies, played a determining role in establishing the price level. The peasant community of the village of Santena thus is not merely the passive object of macrosocial changes but has a distinctive input. Finally the idyllic image of a highly cohesive peasant society free of conflicts collapses in the course of this analysis.

Thus we see again in the work of the Italian microhistorians, particularly Levi, as we saw with the Göttingen group, that microhistory is an extension and not a repudiation of older social science history, a rediscovery of culture and the individuality of persons and small groups as agents of historical change. Nevertheless the societies and cultures to which microhistorical approaches are applicable appear to have both spatial and temporal limits. The charge that microhistorians examine small communities with little or no reference to a broader context is not justified, at least not in the works we have examined. There have been no comparable historical studies, however, of modern urban communities, although work in urban anthropology has been done. All of the works we have discussed deal with a preindustrial world or with the transition of this world into the early stages of industrialization. In part it was possible to deal with villages like Neckarhausen[43] or Santena because they were relatively self-contained and self-sufficient even if they could not fully escape the impact of state administration and of the market. Today Neckarhausen has become in large part a dormitory town whose population commutes to employment or business activities in large population centers.

There is an obvious conflict between certain of the theoretical statements of the microhistorians and their actual research and writing. They rightly stress the discontinuities within history and deduce from them that no grand narrative is possible. But they operate with a largely negative evaluation of modernization. Although they find conflicts and divisions in the premodern communities they study, they regard their passing with a certain degree of nostalgia. That is, they turn to microhistorical communities not simply because the sources exist to study them microhistorically, but also because of a certain dislike for the modern world. Many *Annales* historians may have been similarly motivated to turn to the medieval or early modern world. In a number of recent anthropologically oriented works, such as Eric Wolf's *Europe and the Peoples Without a History*[44] and Sidney Mintz's *Sweetness and Power: Sugar in Modern History*,[45] dealing with the expansion of Europe into the non-Western world, modernization, seen as a destructive force, constitutes a red thread. This is also frequently the case in medieval studies, as in Jacques Le Goff's already mentioned famous essay "Time, Work, and Culture in the Middle Ages," about the origin of the modern concept of time. Although Foucault has emphasized that history has no unity but is marked by "ruptures," his works about insanity, clinics, and prisons assume that the course of modern history is characterized by increasing discipline in daily life. This is also the basic idea in the works of Robert Muchembled, who, like Foucault, links the development of the bureaucratic state in early modern France with the exclusion of nonconformist, marginal groups. And it is also the theme of Norbert Elias's essentially macrohistorical *The Civilizing Process*,[46] which was first published when he was in exile in 1939 and became known only after it was republished in 1969; it traces the disciplining of manners. Here Elias put forward the thesis that, beginning with absolutism, a courtly culture developed that subjected bodily functions such as eating, digesting, and lovemaking, which were formerly practiced relatively uninhibitedly, to new, strict rules and banished them to the private sphere. Certainly discipline has taken on more administratively organized forms in the modern world, but it is doubtful that it was less pervasive in the premodern world that these authors have romanticized to such an extent.

Several criticisms have been raised repeatedly against the microhistorians: (1) that their methods, with their concentration on small-scale history, have reduced history to anecdotal antiquarianism; (2) that they have romanticized past cultures; (3) that because, as already suggested, they purportedly work with relatively stable cultures, they are incapable of dealing with the modern and contemporary worlds marked by rapid change; and (4) in this connection that they are incapable of dealing with politics.

Nevertheless, there have been serious attempts to use microhistorical approaches to deal with political conflicts in the twentieth century. What links the history of everyday life (*All-tagsgeschichte*)[47] in the modern and contemporary period with the microhistory dealing with preindustrial society is the commitment to go beyond impersonal social structures and processes to the concrete life experiences of human beings. Lutz Niethammer, whose primary concern is to explore the everyday world of the working classes, including working-class women, questions how much value price and wage statistics or governmental reports have for understanding the conditions within which people have operated. Here again microhistory is seen not as an alternative to analyses of large-scale social and political processes but as a necessary supplement. At the center of microhistorical investigations stand men and women who have been neglected in the traditional sources. Biographies and memoirs play an important part in the reconstruction of their lives, but obviously in most cases those sources are not available. Here, too, oral history can make a contribution. Oral history has been used particularly to deal with the victims and more recently also the perpetrators of the Holocaust, and most recently the victims and perpetrators of the Stalinist persecutions and massacres. Admittedly there are problems with interviews, particularly when these are gathered several decades later, when the memory of those interviewed has been affected by consequent events and experiences. Nevertheless interviews can be checked against other evidence and other interviews for corroboration. Local history groups have often used oral history methods to communicate the life experiences of common people for their own sakes, but particularly in Germany, and in recent years in the former Soviet Union, these methods have been used as part of a reconstruction of recent history.

There have been questions difficult to answer by traditional methods of political and social analysis. Alf Lüdtke, closely associated with the microhistory group at the Max Planck Institute for History in Göttingen, asked how the historical catastrophes of the Germans in the twentieth century were possible. How does one explain that the working classes, who were organized within a social democratic movement supposedly opposed to German policies leading to war, largely supported the war in 1914 or why indeed in 1933 there was virtually no open resistance against the Nazis among workers but, indeed, widespread support?[48] Older sociological categories of class require careful scrutiny and modification. Carefully conducted in-depth interviews can throw light on the complexity of political and social attitudes. Thus workers imbued with a work ethic and proud of standards of German workmanship performed well in war industries, no matter what their political outlook was. Between the poles of political opposition and support there was a broad spectrum of resistance in the workplace, which took a variety of forms. Two major oral history projects organized by Lutz Niethammer among industrial workers, the first conducted in the Ruhr region,[49] the second in Eastern Germany in the last days of the German Democratic Republic,[50] probed into personal recollections of the Third Reich and the postwar period. In the Soviet Union, beginning with Perestroika, oral historians associated with the Memorial group carried out extensive interviews with survivors of the Stalin era.

Some critics of *Alltagsgeschichte* as it has been practiced in Germany have expressed "the fear that it will normalize the image of the Nazi regime by concentrating on the mundane, everyday aspects of life that continued relatively undisturbed."[51] This was certainly not the intention of the Niethammer team. One example of the critical function of oral history, Christopher Browning's *Ordinary Men: Reserve Police Battalion 101 and the Final Solution in Poland* (1993),[52] is based on interrogations in the 1960s by the state prosecutor's office in Hamburg of 210 former members of the battalion who were involved in the mass executions of Jewish civilians in Poland. Browning's study adds a new perspective to the history of the perpetrators of the Holocaust. Until then the Holocaust had mostly been seen as a vast and complex administrative process, as Raoul Hilberg[53] had described it, carried out from their desks by bureaucrats like Adolf Eichmann, who for Hannah Arendt embodied "the banality of evil."[54] Browning now focused on the role of the little men at the bottom of the hierarchy of the "machinery of destruction" who personally carried out the millions of executions. His account of Reserve Police Battalion 101 showed how middle-aged Hamburg policemen, many of working-class background, without overt anti-Semitic sentiments, were involved in the mass executions in Poland. "There is nothing inherent in the methodology of *Alltagsgeschichte*," Browning notes, "that necessarily diminishes the centrality of the Holocaust in the history of Nazi Germany. On the contrary, I would argue, it is the best method for revealing how deeply mass murder was embedded in the lives of German personnel stationed in occupied eastern Europe."[55]

This leads us once more to the methodological questions raised by the practitioners of microhistory. Their key argument against social science approaches to history was that such history deprived the past of its qualitative aspects and left it without a human face. The question was how the human and the personal side of history could be recaptured. As we saw, Hans Medick found the model for such a history in the "thick description" of Clifford Geertz's cultural anthropology. History, like anthropology, was an interpretive and not a systematic science. Cold analyis was replaced by an immediacy difficult to put into words. It appears to me, however, that the epistemology of thick description contains an unresolvable contradiction. It views the subject of its study as totally different from the observer. It rightly warns against projecting the observer's thought categories onto the observed. Thick description should make the "other" appear to the observer in his/her "otherness." This endows the subject of observation with an element of *objectivity* and makes it appear as an object embedded in reality. On the other hand, this anthropological approach challenged the objectivity of the world. It viewed the other as a text that needed to be read very much as one would read a literary text. A text, however, could be read in a variety of ways. The logical consequence of this approach should have been the elimination of the border between fact and fiction.

But in fact this was not the intent of the microhistorians. In their effort to restore the subjectivity and the individuality of the men and women they studied, they rejected the preoccupation of the social sciences with anonymous structures and processes, but they too in their work as historians assumed that they were confronting a real subject matter. In their effort to come closer to this subject matter, they were quite willing to use the tools of the social sciences. It is striking how, particularly in Germany, microhistorians relied on computer techniques, to be sure with the intent not to establish broad generalizations but rather to discover exceptions to these generalizations. Although the Italians we discussed reflected an anthropological approach much more emphatically than their German colleagues and relied much less on the computer, they nevertheless rejected what they considered to be the methodological relativism of cultural anthropology in the Geertzian manner. In the final analysis microhistory appears not as a negation of a history of broader social contexts but as a supplement to it. The microhistorians have added a sense of concreteness to the study of the past. Using microhistorical methods, Christopher Browning in *Ordinary Men* thus did more than merely detail events within the Holocaust; through his focus on individual perpetrators he also endeavored to add a dimension to their behavior that would not be disclosed by broader generalizations. The Holocaust, Christopher Browning emphasized, is not an abstraction. Nor are the narratives of it, as Hayden White suggested, primarily constructs of the historian.[56] Rather, as Browning notes: "There is a constant dialectical interaction between what the historian brings to the research and how the research affects the historian."[57]

Chapter 10

The "Linguistic Turn": The End of History as a Scholarly Discipline?

I have already referred to postmodern theories of history that take up the questions of the possibility or impossibility of historical knowledge and the forms historical writing should assume in a postmodern age. In this chapter I would like to raise the question of the extent and manner in which postmodern theories of history and language have actually served as the basis of historical writing. These theories proceed from the conviction, to cite Lawrence Stone once more, "that a coherent scientific explanation of change in the past"[1] is no longer possible. But postmodern theories go beyond Stone's formulation in claiming that any coherence is suspect. The basic idea of postmodern theory of historiography is the denial that historical writing refers to an actual historical past. Thus Roland Barthes[2] and Hayden White asserted that historiography does not differ from fiction but is a form of it. Accordingly White tried to demonstrate in *Metahistory: The Historical Imagination in the Nineteenth Century in Europe* (1973), by the example of four historians (Michelet, Tocqueville, Ranke, and Burckhardt) and four philosophers of history (Hegel, Marx, Nietzsche, and Croce), that there are no criteria of truth in historical narratives. Therefore, he argued, there is also no essential difference between the writing of history and the philosophy of history. The critical philological occupation with the sources can, to be sure, discover facts, but any step beyond this toward the construction of a historical account is determined, for White, by aesthetic and ethical, not by scientific considerations. Form and content, he argues, cannot be separated in historical writing. Historians, he continues, have at their disposal a limited number of rhetorical possibilities that predetermine the form and to a certain extent also the content of their account so that, as we saw, "historical narratives are verbal fictions, the contents of which are as much *invented* as *found* and the forms of which have more in common with their counterparts in literature than they have with those in the sciences."[3]

Here White goes far beyond a tradition of historical thought that, from Herodotus to Natalie Davis, recognized both the literary aspects of historical accounts and the role of imagination in constructing them, but nevertheless maintained a faith that these accounts offered insights into a real past involving real human beings. Natalie Davis frankly admitted that invention occupies a crucial place in the reconstruction of the past, but she also insisted that this invention is not the arbitrary creation of the historian but follows the "voices of the past" as they speak to us through the sources.[4] Ranke similarly recognized the role of imagination in reconstrucing the thought processes of his historical actors.

There is therefore a difference between a theory that denies any claim to reality in historical accounts and a historiography that is fully conscious of the complexity of historical knowledge but still assumes that real people had real thoughts and feelings that led to real actions that, within limits, can be known and reconstructed. To be sure, as Patrick Bahners put it, science since Kant has possessed no "material criteria of truth."[5] But Kant and subsequent scientific and social scientific thought, including that of Max Weber, still assumed that there existed a logic of scientific inquiry, which could be communicated and which, while not providing material criteria, offered formal standards for the examination of the world of nature and of men. But even these criteria have been questioned by some contemporary theorists of science.

Among modern and contemporary theorists of science who have challenged the notion that scientific inquiry leads to a progressive understanding of reality, one must distinguish between radical skeptics such as Gaston Bachelard[6] and Paul Feyerabend[7] on the one hand, and historical relativists such as Thomas Kuhn on the other. Bachelard and Feyerabend understand science as a poetic activity for which there is no binding logic or method of inquiry. In *The Structure of Scientific Revolutions* (1960)[8] Kuhn too argued that science cannot be understood as a reflection of an objective world. He did not regard it as fiction, however, but as a historically and culturally conditioned discourse among people who are in agreement about the rules that govern their discourse. For him science is an institutionalized form of scientific inquiry, a way of dealing with reality in a scientific community, whose members agree in regard to strategies of investigation and explanation. Thus Kuhn also questions the relationship of science to reality, but he does not, as do Bachelard and Feyerabend, question the possibility of a rational scientific discourse.

The question of the relationship between knowledge and reality also plays a central role in linguistic theory. Modern science has understood language as a vehicle for the transmission of meaningful knowledge. Logical positivism, as it originated in the Vienna circle in the 1930s and then played an important role in Anglo-American analytical philosophy, strove for a language cleansed of all contradictions and culturally conditioned ambiguities, capable of communicating logical concepts and the results of scientific inquiry. Structuralism subsequently questioned precisely this referential function of language.

For language theory as it was formulated by the Swiss linguist Ferdinand de Saussure in *Course in General Linguistics*,[9] which appeared posthumously in 1916, two related ideas were basic: Language forms a closed autonomous system that possesses a syntactic structure. Moreover, language is not a means for communicating meaning and units of meaning, but on the contrary, meaning is a function of language. Or to put it differently: Man does not use language to transmit his thoughts, but what man thinks is determined by language. Here we have the central idea of the structuralist conception of society and history: Man moves within the framework of structures—in this case linguistic structures—which he does not determine, but which determine him. This conception played an important role in literary theory in the

1950s and 1960s in the "New Criticism" in the United States, and separately in the discussions in France initiated by Roland Barthes and leading to the deconstructionist method of Jacques Derrida.[10] From the perspective of language theory, the text has no reference to an external reality, but is contained within itself. This is true not only of literary but also of historiographical texts. Since texts do not refer to reality, Barthes argues, there is no difference between truth and fiction.[11] The text, moreover, is seen not only independently of its relation to the external world, but also independently of its author. What matters is exclusively the text, not the context in which it originated. The next step, undertaken by Michel Foucault, is to eliminate the author as a relevant factor in the production of texts. And as the author disappears, intentionality and meaning also disappear from the text. For Foucault, history therefore loses its significance. It is a late invention of Western man in what he calls the "classical" phase of modern history, a phase that has already passed. It seems paradoxical that so much of Foucault's writings, chiefly his works about insanity, the clinics, punishment, and sexuality, but also his major theoretical presentations, *The Archeology of Knowledge* and *The Order of Things*, nevertheless reflect a thoroughly historical perspective.

Foucault and Derrida's criticism is directed against the ideological presuppositions that are hidden in every text. The text, they argue, must therefore be liberated from its author. At the same time they radicalize de Saussure's conception of language. For de Saussure, language still possessed a structure; it constituted a system. There still existed a unity between the word (signifier) and the thing to which it referred (signified). For Derrida, this unity no longer exists. Instead he sees an infinite number of signifiers without clear meanings, because there is no Archimedean point from which a clear meaning can be assigned. For historiography this means a world without meaning, devoid of human actors, human volitions or intentions, and totally lacking coherence.

Therefore, if history will be written in the future, it will have to take on completely different forms. This theme is taken up in American discussions of the nature of historical prose. For Hayden White, as we saw, historiography must today be seen as primarily a literary genre following literary criteria. Dominick La Capra, in 1985, called on historiography to recapture the rhetorical quality it had treasured since classical antiquity.[12] In the nineteenth century, as history became a professional discipline and laid claim to being a rigorous science, historians frequently sought to free historical writing from its rhetorical elements. It became fashionable to posit a simple dichotomy between science and rhetoric without understanding that all language, including that of science, has a rhetorical dimension. To cite La Capra, "this tendency, which defines science as the adversary or antithesis of rhetoric, has often been conjoined with a defense of 'plain style' that depends or pretends to be entirely transparent to its object."[13] But there is no such "plain style." In fact, historical writing, even in the nineteenth and twentieth centuries, the age of professionalized scholarship, did not lose its rhetorical or literary qualities. And the great historians recognized this. Thus Ranke emphasized that history was not only science but also art and that the two were inseparable.[14] It is noteworthy that Theodor Mommsen received the Nobel Prize for literature the second time it was given in 1902. Apart from isolated works of quantitative history, there are few examples of a historiography without a significant rhetorical or literary component, not even Robert Fogel and Stanley Engerman's cliometric study of American slavery, *Time on the Cross*, which despite its immense quantitative apparatus tells a story aimed to persuade the reader of their argument that slavery was both cost efficient and humane. Rhetoric, of course, plays an important role even in the documents with which the historian works. The sources, or at least the documents that serve as sources, are themselves linguistic constructs, texts, which, unless they are pure data, use rhetorical strategies to make a point. Statistical data, too, are selected and constructed.

A broad segment of historical thought today takes the above conceptions of language and textuality seriously. The French input into these discussions has profoundly affected literary criticism and theory in the United States. The impact of linguistic theory on historical studies has been even greater in the United States than in France and, in the United States, markedly greater in European than in American history. In the following pages our primary but by no means exclusive emphasis will be on the American discussions, for here the concept of a "linguistic turn"[15] was invented. The central element of this "turn" consists in the recognition of the importance of language or discourse in the constitution of societies. The social structures and processes that were seen as the determinants of a society and culture are now increasingly viewed rather as products of culture understood as a communicative community. This stress on the centrality of language has entered into a good deal of recent scholarship in political, social, cultural, and intellectual history. But while certain writers drew very radical consequences from linguistic theory and reduced history to semiotics, in which society was seen as culture and culture as a "web of significance" resembling a literary text and defying reduction to a reality beyond the text, other historians saw language as a tool for approaching social and cultural reality.

The cultural anthropologist Clifford Geertz has provided recent historical thought with perhaps the most important stimulus toward a semiotic approach to culture. "Believing with Max Weber," he writes, "that man is an animal suspended in webs of significance he himself has spun, I take culture to be those webs, and the analysis of it to be therefore not an experimental science in search of law but an interpretive one in search of meaning."[16] But he gives the concept "web of significance" a very different meaning from the one Weber gave it. For Weber this constituted a repudiation of the positivist method, which restricts itself to the empirical observation of reality. Reality, Weber agrees with Kant, is accessible only through the mediation of the logical categories of the mind. But for him this by no means signifies a repudiation of a rigorous logic of social scientific inquiry. In fact for Weber "objectivity" constitutes the cornerstone of social scientific inquiry.[17] Objectivity here does not relate to an "object" in the external world but to the methodology of the social sciences by means of which this world is studied. The logic of this methodology has its roots in the intellectual history of the Western world since Greek antiquity; its validity, however, extends to rational thought in all cultures. We have already cited his affirmation that logical argumentation in the social sciences must be convincing to a Chinese as well as a Western mind. The

Weberian notion of the "ideal type" does not negate but rather presupposes the notion that there are real social structures and processes that form the subject of social scientific inquiry. It recognizes that a purely empirical approach is not possible; nevertheless it assumes that one can approach social reality by testing the "ideal types" against empirical findings. For Weber, moreover, social science studies the macrohistorical and macrosocial structures and processes that form societies. This emphasis on clear concepts and explicit theories, as we saw, forms the basis of a great deal of social science-oriented thought including the German school of "Historical Social Science" of Hans-Ulrich Wehler and Jürgen Kocka, which cultural historians increasingly reject as objectivistic.

Despite his invocation of Weber, Geertz thus goes in a totally different direction. What anthropologists do, he tells us, "is not a matter of methods" but of "thick description." Thick description as an alternative to method rests on a conception of culture that Geertz defines as "semiotic."[18] From this perspective, a culture possesses the characteristics of a language and, like a language, constitutes a "system." This makes interpretation possible because each act and each expression has a symbolic value that reflects the culture as a whole. Thick description involves the direct confrontation with the symbolic expressions of the culture free of any theory-guided questions that, by means of abstractions, threaten to deprive the manifestations of the culture of their vitality. On the surface there thus appears to be a similarity between the anthropological confrontation with the subject of study through thick description and the hermeneutic approach of classical historicism, which seeks to "understand" its subject free of abstractions. But this similarity is deceptive. Hermeneutics assumes there is a common ground between the observer and the observed that makes understanding possible. Geertz on the contrary views the subject he observes as totally different. To reduce the subject to terms we can understand means to distort it rather than grasp it in its otherness.

In the previous chapter I discussed Geertz's impact on the history of everyday life and on microhistory. Here we are interested in the semiotic approach to cultural history. Geertz's approach, so frequently invoked in recent cultural history, presents a number of problems for a critical history. Not only is he not a historian but he has little understanding for history. His famous essay on "The Balinese Cockfight"[19] is a prime example of his approach. The reactions of the audience at the cockfight reflect a culture, seen as a semiotic system, that is both integrated and stable, forming a whole. Gerrtz does not see the culture within the framework of social processes taking place in Balinese society; nor does he consider social divisions and social conflicts. Thus despite his avowed purpose of avoiding systematization and concentrating instead on the unique manifestation of behavior, he resorts to the very macro conception of society that he rejects. And this results in methodological irrationalism. The interpretation of symbols cannot be tested empirically. The "meaning" of the foreign culture confronts the anthropologist directly. This is to prevent the introduction of a subjective bias, which supposedly colors the work of both analytical social scientists working with theory-guided questions and the traditional historians who believed they could understand the subject of their study. But in fact there are no mechanisms of control in Geertz's interpretation of cultures. The result is the reintroduction of the anthropologist's subjectivity or imagination into his subject matter. The French sociologist Pierre Bourdieu, in his study of Maghreb culture, has offered a more differentiated view of culture than Geertz. His approach, which stresses the economic and social context of culture but recognizes the symbolic character of these relationships, reflects his early beginnings in Marxist thought but also his reinterpretation of Marxism. He agrees with Max Weber that in the final analysis concepts of honor enter into economic relationships to form a cultural substratum. The culture can no longer be seen as a self-contained text, but must be seen in a political, social, and economic context of change that must to be approached through its symbols.

Two modifications of a Geertzian approach and its application to a historical theme might be mentioned here, Marshall Sahlin's essay on the death of Captain Cook[20] and Robert Darnton's *The Great Cat Massacre.*[21] Sahlin portrays the interaction of two different cultures, the Polynesian culture of Hawaii and the Western culture of the British explorers that impinges on it, each with a logic of its own. He then seeks to explain the murder of Cook by the Hawaiians in terms of the religious code of Hawaiian culture and at the same time places it within the framework of the expansion of Western capitalism. Thus text and context, which have been separated by Geertz, are rejoined. But the reconstruction of Hawaiian culture, like Geertz's study of Balinese culture, has few mechanisms of empirical control. Darnton, on the basis of an account by a printer apprentice thirty years after the fact, recounts the story of a ritual killing of cats carried out as a symbolic act of revolt by printers against their employer and his wife. According to Chartier, Darnton uses culture in Geertz's terms as "an historically transmitted pattern of meanings embodied in symbols, a system of inherited conceptions expressed in symbolic form by means of which men communicate, perpetuate and develop their knowledge about and attitudes towards life."[22] Similarly to Le Roy Ladurie in the *Carnival in Romans*,[23] Darnton interprets the ritualism of the massacre in terms of sexual aggression, through which the economically and socially exploited symbolically confront their superiors. As Geertz does in the "Balinese Cockfight," Darnton seeks to recapture a folk culture. At the same time he places this text within the broader context of the conflict that resulted from the economic transformation of the printing trade under the pressures of capitalist modernization. But the question remains whether through the thick description of the cat massacre, reminiscent of the Balinese cockfight, one can actually reconstruct a culture in all its complexity.

Although Geertz has been frequently invoked by cultural historians, he has in fact proved to be of limited value to their work beyond contributing to the turn away from what he calls "an experimental science in search of law [to] an interpretive one in search of meaning."[24] In this search for meaning, language became an important semiotic tool. Thus a "linguistic turn" has occurred in diverse areas of social and cultural history, but nowhere has the belief that language refers to reality been given up, as it was in the reinterpretation of Saussurean linguistic theory by Barthes, Derrida, and Lyotard.

I shall briefly examine several orientations in recent social and cultural history that assign a key place to language or discourse not as a substitute for social reality but as a guide to it:

Of these the one furthest removed from cultural anthropology and most closely akin to traditional forms of intellectual history is found in the studies in the history of political thought by J. G. A. Pocock, Quentin Skinner, and Reinhart Koselleck. In many ways they resemble traditional intellectual histories as represented in the classical histories of ideas of Benedetto Croce, Friedrich Meinecke, R. G. Collingwood, and Arthur Lovejoy. They, too, proceed hermeneutically in studying the texts left by the great political theorists. They see these texts as containing authorial intentions, and in their view it continues to be the task of the historian, as it was of their classical predecessors, to fathom the meanings of these texts. Since ideas can no longer be understood primarily as the creations of great minds but must be seen as part of the discourse of the intellectual community within which they were articulated, Pocock[25] and Skinner[26] turn to the continuity of Western political thought from Florentine humanism to the emergence of a concept of civil society in the Enlightenment. Both use the term "Political Thought" in the titles of their books. They distinguish themselves from traditional intellectual history by their emphasis on discursive structures that persisted over long periods of time. In viewing texts as vehicles for the communication of consciously held ideas, they differ from postmodern conceptions of language and discourse. Ideas, they maintain, continue to be conceived and articulated by thinking human beings who are aware of what they are doing and yet reflect and articulate within the framework of the discourse of their community. The discourse presupposes a community of relatively autonomous actors who can communicate with each other because they speak a common language through which they can affect the political and social world. This conception of discourse is not far removed from Jürgen Habermas's theory of communicative action.[27] The discourse contributes to the formation of political reality, by which in turn it is also affected. Reinhart Koselleck[28] goes further than Pocock and Skinner in using the analysis of discourse as a means of reconstructing not merely the history of political thought but also that of political and social structures. Together with Werner

Conze and Otto Brunner, two of the most important German social historians, Koselleck in 1973 launched a seven-volume encyclopedia of "Basic Historical Concepts."[29] In lengthy articles, some over a hundred pages long, authors examined in depth the meaning and transformation of key political and social concepts in Germany in the period between 1750 and 1850. The assumption was that through an analysis of the "politico-social language" of the period insights could be gained into the social and political transformation from premodern to modern institutions and thought patterns that took place in this crucial period.

Moving closer to an analysis of political history that stresses symbols rather than concepts are the works of Lynn Hunt, François Furet, Maurice Agulhon, Mona Ozouf, and William Sewell on the revolutionary changes in France. One should mention here Régine Robin's analyses[30] in the early 1970s of the language of the *cahiers de doléances* in the early stages of the French Revolution and the semantics of political terms such as "nation," "*citoyen*," and "*seigneur*." As Lynn Hunt explains in the introduction to her *Politics, Culture and Class in the French Revolution* (1984), this work conceived in 1976 began as "a social history of Revolutionary politics" but "increasingly turned into a cultural analysis in which the political structures . . . became but one part of the story."[31] Hunt by no means denies the role of social structures and processes in bringing about the French Revolution, but in her opinion these are not enough to explain the Revolution. The politics of the Revolution was not a mere expression of underlying economic and social interests. Rather, through their language, their imagery, and their everyday political activities, the revolutionaries had participated in the reshaping of society. In this way they had contributed to the creation of new social and political conditions. The decisive factor in the formation of the political culture of the French Revolution were for Hunt the symbolic gestures, images, and rhetoric of the revolutionaries. Hunt here expresses her debt to Furet, Agulhon, and Ozouf. Furet, originally a Marxist, had in the 1960s and early 1970s advocated a social science orientation with a strong quantitative bend. In the 1970s, as we saw, he took issue not only with the hardline Marxist analysis of the French Revolution by Albert Soboul,[32] but also with such critics of a Marxist position as Alfred

Cobban[33] and George Taylor,[34] who considered Soboul's[35] or Lefebvre's[36] conception of a bourgeois revolution inadequate but continued to seek economic and social explanations. Furet now sought to place the Revolution in the framework of a political culture in which ideas played a significant role.[37] The concept of a political culture was developed further in Agulhon's[38] and Ozouf's[39] studies of revolutionary festivals, symbols, and rhetoric, which created a republican consciousness in broad segments of the population.

In a somewhat similar manner, William Sewell, in *Work and Revolution in France: The Language of Labor from the Old Regime to 1848* (1980),[40] deals with the decisive role of language in shaping the revolutionary consciousness of workers. His focus is on the revolutionary movement that led to the events of 1848 in Marseilles. He points to the broad consensus in recent studies that the most important impulses for strike actions and outbreaks of violence in France, England, Germany, and the United States in the early decades of industrialization did not come from industrial workers, as Marxists assumed, but from artisans. The revolution of 1848 thus took place within the framework of perceptions that were deeply rooted in a preindustrial, corporatist world. Thus Sewell notes that "although we obviously cannot hope to experience what nineteenth-century workers experienced . . . we can, with a little ingenuity, search out in the surviving records the symbolic forms through which they experienced their world." And "because communication is not limited to speech and writing, we must also seek out the intelligible forms of many other activities, events and institutions: of the practices of artisans' organizations, of rituals and ceremonies, of the shape of political demonstrations, of legal regulations, or of details of the organization of production" in which "the symbolic content and the conceptual coherence of working-class experiences" are reflected.[41]

While Sewell stresses the role of symbols, Gareth Stedman Jones and Thomas Childers concentrate more directly on language. Stedman Jones in particular emphasizes the extent to which language not only expresses but constitutes social reality. Yet all three accept the existence of real social structures and processes and see in language a tool for examining them. Like

Thompson, Stedman Jones deals with the constitution of the English working class. He acknowledges Thompson's contribution in freeing the idea of class consciousness from its immediate link to an economic base. But more specifically than Thompson, he locates the essential elements of class consciousness in the language of class. Thompson's conception of working-class experience needs to be refined because this experience is embedded in a language that gives it its structure.[42] Thus conventional conceptions that have interpreted Chartism in terms of class consciousness are inadequate if they overlook the extent to which Chartism was embedded not in social structures but in a given political language. The rise and decline of Chartism, Stedman Jones argues, was determined less by the economic misery or the social transformations occasioned by the Industrial Revolution than by the political language with which the supporters of Chartism interpreted their economic and social deprivation. By no means does this mean that economic conditions and social transformations are to be neglected in the analysis of Chartism as a political movement, any less than Sewell neglected them in his treatment of the revolutionary movement that led to the 1848 uprisings in Marseilles, but they must be understood by means of the language and the discourse that shaped the political consciousness of workers.

This same viewpoint is present in Thomas Childers's essay "The Social Language of Politics in Germany,"[43] in which he relates his own thoughts to those of Hunt, Stedman Jones, Sewell, and Scott. His immediate concern in the essay is the political culture of the Weimar Republic, which led to the rise of the Nazis. His starting point is the controversy between social science-oriented historians such as Hans Ulrich Wehler and Jürgen Kocka, who explained Nazism in terms of the belated and incomplete democratization of Germany in an age of industrialization, and their English critics Geoff Eley and David Blackbourn, who questioned the thesis that modernization in Germany differed substantially from that in other countries. Both theses are inadequate in Childers's sight because they rely too exclusively on economic and social factors. Childers does not deny the importance of these factors but believes they must be seen within the framework of the political language employed. This language reflects actual social distinctions but also shapes the political and social consciousness of the classes that speak it and hear it. Childers therefore sets out to examine the vocabulary used by political parties, interest groups, governmental authorities, and individuals in order to delineate the political consciousness of the contending sides. To do this he analyzes the language used in "day-to-day partisan literature and activities—leaflets, pamphlets, posters, speeches, and meetings—for every national campaign and a great many local contests from 1919 to Adolf Hitler's assumption of power in January 1933"[44] in order to reconstruct the political discourse of the time. Like Sewell and Stedman Jones, he challenges the "ontological priority of economic events" without neglecting the role of social and economic conditions.

Joan Scott in her essays in *Gender and the Politics of History* (1988), at least in her theoretical formulations, advocates a position considerably more radical with regard to the primacy of speech than any of the historians whom we have just discussed in her attempt to lay the foundations for a "feminist reading of history." Unlike these historians, she explicitly endorses Derrida's conception of language and Foucault's conception of power. She agrees with Derrida that traditional language posits a hierarchical order that consistently over time has resulted in the subjugation of women.[45] Similarly she accepts Foucault's notion that knowledge constitutes power and domination. But while Derrida's position posits a linguistic determinism that leaves little space for an active political program, Scott bases a feminist politics on a Derridean theory of language. She convincingly argues that gender in a social and political in contrast to a biological sense is not given by nature but "constituted" by language. She then criticizes Stedman Jones because "he treats language simply as a vehicle for communicating ideas rather than as a system of meaning or a process of signification." Further, she notes critically that "he slips back to the notion that 'language' reflects a 'reality' external to it, rather than being constitutive of that reality."[46] This led Sewell in an otherwise very positive review of the essays to note that "Scott has accepted Derridian and literary deconstructionism too uncritically, and has not sufficiently considered the problems inherent in appropriating a theoretical vocabulary initially developed in philosophy and literary criticism for the study of history." Thus "she argues that any distinction between history and literature vanishes."[47] When I recently communicated with her on this question, she explicated her position by writing me: "My argument is not that reality is 'merely' a text, but rather that reality can only be attained through language. So social and political structures aren't denied, rather they must be studied through their linguistic articulation. And Derrida is useful for such a study. . . . "[48] Except for the recourse to Derrida this is a perspective not essentially different from that of Stedman Jones, whom she criticizes. As a matter of fact, in her studies of the role of leading women who represented a feminist viewpoint in the revolutionary movements in France,[49] Scott assigns a role to language very similar to that assigned by Sewell and Stedman Jones.

. . .

In conclusion: Linguistic theory, as it has been developed in French literary theory from Barthes to Derrida and Lyotard, contains an element that in my opinion must be taken very seriously and that has applications to historical thought and writing. The participants in this discussion have rightly raised the point that history taken as a whole contains no immanent unity or coherence, that every conception of history is a construct constituted through language, that human beings as subjects have no integrated personality free of contradictions and ambivalences, and that every text can be read and interpreted in different ways because it expresses no unambiguous intentions. Foucault and Derrida have with good justification pointed out the political implications of language and the hierarchical relations of power inherent in it. These contradictions, which permeate all of human life, force the observer to "deconstruct" every text, in order to lay bare its ideological elements. Every reality is not only communicated through speech and discourse but in a very fundamental way is also constituted by them.

Nevertheless this philosophy of language lends itself better to literary criticism than to historical writing. For historical accounts, even if they use forms of narrative that are closely patterned on literary models, still claim to portray or reconstruct an actual past to a greater extent than is the case in fictional litera-

ture. Despite the invocation of postmodern linguistic theory by
Joan Scott and by Lynn Hunt in her volume *New Cultural History*,[50] social and cultural historians have moved in a very different direction. The "linguistic turn" in historical studies over the
past decade and a half has been part of an effort to break the
determinism inherent in older socioeconomic approaches and to
emphasize the role of cultural factors, among which language
occupies a key place. But as Stedman Jones notes, this is not a
matter of replacing a social with a linguistic interpretation, but of
examining how the two are related.[51] Linguistic analysis has
proven to be an important supplementary tool in recent studies of
political, social, and cultural history. Yet in general, although the
historians with whom we have dealt in this chapter have emphasized the impact of language, rhetoric, and symbolic behavior on
political and social consciousness and action, the extreme position that "reality does not exist, that only language exists" (Foucault)[52] has been shared by few. Most historians would agree with
Carroll Smith-Rosenberg that "while linguistic differences structure society, social differences structure language."[53]

Chapter 11

From the Perspective of the 1990s

In 1979 Lawrence Stone, in his now famous article "The Revival of Narrative," cast doubts on the older social science model of historical studies and endorsed the new orientation toward anthropology and semiotics. In 1991, in a note, "History and Post-Modernism,"[1] again in *Past and Present*, he expressed his concern about the radical direction historical discourse had taken since then. As we remember, in "The Revival of Narrative" he had heralded "the end of the attempt to produce a coherent scientific explanation of change in the past." He now saw a triple threat to history: from postmodernism, from linguistics, and cultural and symbolic anthropology, and from the New Historicism. All three agree in dealing with political, institutional, and social practice as "discursive sets of symbolic systems or codes." "Texts thus become a mere hall of mirrors reflecting nothing but each other, and throwing no light upon the 'truth,' which does not exist." From these perspectives, in the final analysis, "the real is as imagined as the imaginary."[2]

Stone's warnings were promptly challenged by the British social and cultural historian Patrick Joyce. The "real," he admitted, "can be said to exist independently of our representations of it," but he insisted that "history is never present to us in anything but a discursive form." The major advance of postmodernism, in his view, was the recognition that "there is no overarching coherence evident in either the polity, the economy or the social system" and that "there is no underlying structure" to which the texts from which our understanding of the historical context emerges "can be referred."[3]

But from the perspective of the 1990s, Joyce's position seems much less convincing than it did a decade earlier. Of course, even in the 1980s the postmodern approach as defined by Joyce by no means had a monopoly. The "linguistic turn" that occupied the pages of the *American Historical Review* and other American journals in the second half of the 1980s did not have the same fascination for historians outside North America, even in France, although the concepts on which it rested originated in large part in French literary theory from Barthes to Derrida. We have already noted the limited effect radically formulated theories of linguistic determinism had on historical writing, even on writers such as Gareth Stedman Jones, William Sewell, Lynn Hunt, and Thomas Childers, who saw in discourse a significant key to historical understanding. Stone could argue convincingly "that it is impossible to think of a major historical work written from a thoroughly postmodernist perspective and using postmodernist language and vocabulary."[4] Perhaps Simon Schama's *Dead Certainties: Unwarranted Speculations*[5] and Jonathan Spence's *The Question of Hu*[6] went farthest in the direction of a historiography that consciously dissolved the border between scholarly history and historical novel.

At the threshold between the 1980s and the 1990s stand the revolutionary changes in the Soviet Union and in Eastern Europe. In retrospect there may be explanations for these changes; at the time they were largely unforeseen. In significant ways they undermined the self-confidence of the older social sciences, which believed in the possibility of coherent social explanation, as well as of the new cultural history, which largely ignored the political context of the culture of everyday life. The collapse of communism appeared to confirm the predictions of Western advocates of capitalism who, like Francis Fukuyama, were convinced that the pressures of economic modernization would necessarily lead to corporate market economies and representative democracy. America would thus become the model for the world—though the events following 1989 soon disproved these prophesies. Notwithstanding these predictions, few analysts had expected the immanent collapse of the Soviet system. While reforms in the Soviet Union and its Eastern European client states in the wake of Gorbachev's Perestroika had been anticipated, it was generally expected that they would occur within the framework of the socialist system and would leave the international order dominated by the two superpowers intact. Largely unexpected was the unification of Germany as well as the dissolution of the Soviet Union. As a matter of fact, it was generally believed that internal reforms in the Eastern states and the Soviet Union would normalize relations between the two blocks. As regards Germany, this normalization would have meant that unification would lose its urgency. Unforeseen were the new forms of domestic and especially ethnic violence that followed the events of 1989 to 1991, not only in the successor states of the Soviet Union and of Yugoslavia, but also in the Moslem world and in Subsaharan Africa. The changes in the world order raised significant questions for historical thought and practice that made it difficult for historical inquiry to follow the lines it had followed previously.

Undoubtedly the persistence of cultural traditions became increasingly apparent. The concepts of modernization that had dominated a great deal of social science thought in the 1950s and 1960s and continued to play an important role later were difficult to reconcile with the revival of religious fundamentalism and ethnic particularism. Seventy years of Communist rule had not eliminated ancient religious traditions. Similarly fundamentalism in its Moslem, Protestant, Orthodox Jewish, and Hindu forms appeared to be a reaction against the impact that modernization had on traditional beliefs and mores. All this seemed to make anthropological approaches to history even more urgent. At the same time the failure of the Communist regimes to keep in step with the structural changes in the modern economies undoubtedly contributed to their collapse. Beginning in the 1960s the scientific-technical revolution was a major theme in theoretical discussions in the Eastern Bloc, but this revolution, which led to a postindustrial information economy in the West, failed to occur in the Soviet Bloc. The Soviet Union and its client states collapsed in part because of their inability to face the challenges of a modernizing society. Paradoxically the events of

1989–91 not only discredited basic Marxist concepts and made a shambles of Marxist teleology but also lent themselves well to a Marxist analysis. As an ideology and a utopia Marxism had turned out to be a bad dream. Yet in a significant way, to use Marx's concepts, the collapse of the Soviet system demonstrated the revolt of the changing means of production against the outdated conditions of production. The ideology and the dictatorship contributed to the rigidification of a system that could not respond to the changing exigencies of the time. While these observations lend support to a structural and a cultural approach to the history of the recent past, they also raise the question, sometimes neglected in recent historical studies, of the role of politics. Undoubtedly personalities such as Gorbachev and Yeltsin affected the course of events, even if they did so within definite structural constraints. All this seems to call not for the abandonment of older patterns of social, cultural, and political history but for a broadening of the perspective and methods of historical inquiry.

Looking at the discussions and the publications of the last several years, one is struck by both continuities and ruptures. Themes that dominated in the 1980s continue to receive attention today. The disillusion with quantitative history continues. The interest in anthropological history flourishes, as demonstrated by the founding of the German-language journal *Historische Anthropologie* in 1993. The Italian journal *Quaderni Storici* has been a pioneer in these studies. The Russian journal *Odysseus* reflects similar interests. The programs of the annual meetings of the American Historical Association, but also the tables of contents of major journals in the United States, demonstrate the fascination with the themes of "class, gender, and ethnicity," reflecting current social and political pressures in the United States and elsewhere. Nevertheless, there is also a marked retreat in recent historical studies from the pronounced culturalism of the 1980s to new concerns with the modern and contemporary world, away from the preoccupation with the early modern and medieval European world, which had been the subject of a great deal of the new cultural history.

The pronounced reorientation of the *Annales* was indicative of the change of mood in the 1990s. As I have mentioned, in

January 1994 the journal dropped its subtitle *Economies. So-ciétés. Civilisations*, which it had used since the immediate post-war period, and replaced it by *Histoire, Sciences Sociales*. The change in name was the result of intense discussions among its editors since the late 1980s, reflected in an editorial in the January-February issue of 1994 announcing the change.[7] An important editorial in 1988 had already suggested that history and the social sciences were entering into a deep crisis.[8] The change of name, however, demonstrated an awareness that the political and social conditions had changed fundamentally in recent years. The subtitle *Economies. Sociétés. Civilisations* had consciously eliminated politics as a prime concern of history and with it downgraded the role of narratives. Now in the face of the momentous changes at the end of the 1980s, politics was rediscovered and with it the role of personalities. The new title was intended to include politics once more. And in the realm of politics, as François Furet's reappraisal of the French Revolution indicated, ideas and persons again played a decisive role. The *Annales* in choosing the new title by no means intended to exclude society and culture from historical consideration, but wished rather to reestablish the political context in which they occurred. They now wished to pay greater attention to present-day problems. The close relationship between history and the social sciences was to remain, but economics, sociology, and political science were to regain the position they had lost in the post-World War II *Annales*, which did not mean a return to oldtime diplomatic history nor to economics working with abstract models separated from a broader political and social context. The *Annales* issues of the 1990s reflected this reorientation. Problems of the contemporary world, which had also played an important role in the journal in the 1930s, resurfaced. Recent issues have dealt with such diverse contemporary concerns as the opening of the Soviet archives, the organization of labor in Japan, the confrontation with the Vichy past, the modernization of traditional societies, aspects of the development of American capitalism, politics and AIDS in Zaire, religious violence in India and Algeria today, but also traditional topics going back to the early modern and the medieval period, such as the centralization of state power in Asian and European societies, urban sociability in the Middle Ages, the development of credit networks, finances, and accountability in a mercantile economy, "illness, faith and the imaginary" in the Middle Ages, utopias in twelfth-century Byzantium, and Jewish communal life from the seventeenth to the twentieth century.

The renewed turn to politics and to the social sciences in the *Annales* and elsewhere does not represent a repudiation of older interests and concerns but rather a broadening of the scope of historical studies. Important aspects of the postmodernist critique of historical reason remain in place. The faith in the grand narratives focused on the modernization of the Western world as the culmination of a coherent historical process is irredeemably lost. Reflecting on the history of the *Annales*, Jacques Revel, one of its longtime editors and since 1995 director of the Ecole des Hautes Etudes en Sciences Sociales, in a volume published in 1995 that tries to reassess the status of historical studies today, writes that the vision of "total" or "global" history that occupied three generations of *Annales* historians has been laid to rest.[9] But history has not been reduced to a multiplicity of unrelated entities. We have seen how the microhistorians in Italy and Germany, despite their concentration on the local, never lost sight of broader historical and political contexts. In fact they believed that the concentration on the local, which always differed from the "normal,"[10] made it possible to test generalizations. No matter how hard microhistorians challenged Marxist, Weberian, or Rostowan conceptions of the transformation of the modern world, they failed to escape from a notion of modernization, now seen mostly as a destructive force that impinges on the microscale of local history. The main theme of microhistorical studies in fact has been the impact of state, economy, and church on the countryside in an age of incipient modernization.

Finally, postmodernism had raised important epistemological questions that radically challenged the possibility of objective knowledge. Not only was the coherence of history questioned but also the coherence of the author and of the text. The immediacy of historical knowledge was denied; this, however, was nothing new but went back at least to Kant. Hayden White's assertion that history always assumed a narrative form and thus shared the qualities of literary texts, was generally accepted, but not his conclusion that history, like all literature, is therefore essentially a "fiction-making operation." Roger Chartier commented in 1993 that "even if the historian writes in a 'literary manner,' he does not produce literature."[11] His labor is dependent on archival research and, while his sources do not present themselves in an unambiguous form, they are nevertheless subject to criteria of reliability. The historian is always on the outlook for forgery and falsification and thus operates with a notion of truth, however complex and incomplete the road to it may be.

All this points not to a new paradigm but to an expanded pluralism. It is apparent that the "loss of history"[12] so widely noted after World War II is not characteristic of the present mood. In Germany the sense of loss is attributable to the discrediting of national traditions; elsewhere, it stemmed from the belief that the modern world spelled the end of traditional values and forms of community. Temporarily in the early 1970s history course offerings in the United States, Great Britain, West Germany, and elsewhere, but certainly not in France or Poland, were replaced by social studies courses, and at least in the English-speaking world the social sciences frequently took a strongly ahistorical stance. The number of history students declined drastically in the United States. But this trend was reversed in the 1980s. History offerings at the universities became more diversified, particularly in the United States, to include gender and ethnic studies as well as the study of non-Western societies and cultures.[13] Historical journals, books, and TV presentations proliferated. The commemorations of the fiftieth anniversaries of the liberation of the concentration camps and the end of World War II were indicators of the intense concern with history. Thus the cataclysmic changes in Europe since 1989 appear to have strengthened rather than weakened interest in the past.

Concluding Remarks

I. The "End of History"?

Repeatedly in recent years the opinion has been expressed that we are living in a posthistorical age, that history as we have known it has come to an end.[1] What is meant is obviously not that time will hence stand still, but that there is no longer the possibility of a grand narrative that gives history coherence and meaning. The idea that has been central to Judaeo-Christian faith since Biblical antiquity has been questioned, namely, that history has a transmundane purpose and direction. The Enlightenment secularized this faith and placed the eschaton of history into the process of human history itself. It celebrated the civilization of the modern West as the high point and the approaching fulfillment of a desirable social order in which human freedom and culture would be guaranteed. Most recently Francis Fukuyama has reiterated this optimistic belief.[2]

The nineteenth century marked the high point of confidence in the beneficence of historical development, yet at the same time it marked the beginning of a deep uncertainty about the quality of modern culture. The early critique came from voices uneasy about the very notions of scientific rationality, technical progress, and human rights so highly valued by the civilization of the nineteenth century. They included not only thinkers nostalgic for a premodern, preindustrial world, but also some who wanted to go beyond it. This often antidemocratic critique turned against the vision of a world in which enlightenment would free men and women from the age-old bane of subordination, deprivation, and violence. What troubled Kierkegaard, Nietzsche, Burckhardt, Dostoyevsky, and Baudelaire was less the violence and injustice inherent in the modern European world, which had disturbed other thinkers like Alexander Herzen, than what they felt to be the vulgarization of values in the process of massification and the decline of heroism that accompanied it. Kierkegaard on the eve of the 1848 revolutions bewailed modern man's loss of capability for heroic violence.[3] Outdated elites had been eliminated in the political and social transformation that had created the business world of the nineteenth century supposedly without new culturally creative elites taking their place. Science and technology were seen by an ever broader segment of thinkers as the ultimate consequences of a process of rationalization that destroyed the elements of myth and poetry that had endowed life with meaning and now confronted man with nothingness and the absurdity of existence. Proceeding from this pessimism regarding modern civilization, historical thought went in two contradictory directions: One was consciously elitist and antidemocratic; its later representatives such as Ernst Jünger and Carl Schmitt fantasized about the renewal of a national community (*Volksgemeinschaft*) in a world of technological war and violence. A second included thinkers after 1945 who, to be sure, rejected this elitist attitude but took over many of its criticisms of science and technology as a part of their critique of capitalism, thinkers who saw in modern science and technology instruments for the destruction of a humane world.

In the process several ideas central to the modern conception of history lost their credibility. The understanding of history that emerged in the eighteenth century and became dominant in the nineteenth rested on several assumptions. One was the notion that there was one history, *die Geschichte*, that permitted a continuous narrative of historical development. Ranke in 1824 had still entitled his first work *Histories of the Latin and Germanic Peoples*, although he in fact pursued one grand narrative, the emergence of the modern state system at the turn to the sixteenth century. Another idea was that there existed certain key institutions, primarily the state, that occupied the central role in the narrative. J. G. Droysen could thus distinguish between "history" (*die Geschichte*) and "transactions" (*Geschäfte*),[4] the latter comprising the many aspects of everyday life and the many persons who were considered irrelevant to the great flow of history. Finally, as already noted, there was the firm belief expressed by Hegel, Ranke, Comte, Marx, and many others that there was only one truly historical culture and society, that of the Occident.

All three notions succumbed to the criticism of the twentieth century. The idea of the unity of history was challenged relatively early in the twentieth century by Oswald Spengler,[5] Arnold Toynbee,[6] and others, who wanted to write a comparative history of "high cultures." But this distinction between "civilized" and "primitive" peoples was rejected by cultural anthropology along with the image of "Peoples without a History."[7] And increasingly, segments of the population that had been ignored by historians demanded a place in history. The focus of history was thus expanded to include not only the centers of power but also the margins of society, giving birth to microhistory and the notion of many histories. Yet the recognition that it is no longer possible to find a grand narrative that gives direction to history does not mean that history, as has often been lamented, has lost all meaning. History continues to be a powerful means by which groups and persons define their identity. In the place of one meaningful process there is now a pluralism of narratives touching on the existential life experiences of many different groups.

While this book has argued for the legitimacy of microhistory, it has also shown how the latter has never been able to escape the framework of larger structures and transformations in which this history takes place. As we saw, almost all microhistorians have had to confront processes of modernization through their impact on the small social groupings to which they dedicated themselves. The concept of modernization has lost its normative aspects, yet it continues to denote processes that are operative in the modern world. The historian is aware of the extent to which modernization is not a unitary process but expresses itself differently in differing social settings with different cultural traditions. At best modernization becomes an ideal type by which concrete changes can be measured against concrete conditions. Nevertheless, the present state of historical consciousness, far from having put an "end" to history, has led to increasing sophistication in which both the broader context and the individual diversities have their place.

2. The End of History as a Scholarly Enterprise?

Our survey of historical studies in the twentieth century has attempted to show that the disrepute into which the "noble dream"[8] of historical objectivity has fallen has by no means led to a decline in serious historical inquiry. Instead it has led to a diversification of approaches and often to an increase in scholarly sophistication. Certain things have become increasingly obvious. The assurance with which professional historians after Ranke had assumed that immersion in the sources would assure a perception of the past that corresponded to reality has long been modified. However, historians have not given up the basic commitment to historical honesty that inspired Ranke and his colleagues. As historians in recent times have increasingly recognized the limits of objectivity, they have in some ways become more aware of the biases that compromise their honesty than did the "scientific" school in the Rankean tradition, which labored under the illusion that objective knowledge was possible. In many ways history as a "craft" has preserved many of the methodological procedures on which the older history rested. The historian is still bound by his or her sources, and the critical apparatus with which he or she approaches them remains in many ways the same. Nevertheless we view these sources more cautiously. We have become more aware of the extent to which they do not directly convey reality but are themselves narrative constructs that reconstruct these realities, not willy-nilly, but guided by scholarly findings and by a scholarly discourse.

The scope of historical studies has increased dramatically in the past several decades, not only in terms of the groups and individuals studied but also of the themes and questions that interest the historian. The themes, which often touch on existential aspects of life, have required new scholarly strategies that, as we have seen, have placed new emphases on the interpretation of meaningful relationships that lose their qualitative aspects when they are subjected to impersonal analytical categories. Here imagination and empathy enter, but an imagination that, as Natalie Davis stressed, is guided by the "voices of the past."[9] The critical attitude toward scientific rationality has led some historians to deny any essential difference between history and fiction. Various writers have argued that history is indistinguishable from myth and that the attempt of historians since the professionalization of historical studies to forsake rhetoric for scholarly inquiry is a mistake that should be reversed.[10] Frank Ankersmit has argued that historians should frankly recognize that their discourse is metaphorical, and that coherence does not have its source "in reality" but "in the language we use for speaking about it."[11] Peter Novick has in my opinion rightly maintained that objectivity is unattainable in history; the historian can hope for nothing more than plausibility.[12] But plausibility obviously rests not on the arbitrary invention of an historical account but involves rational strategies of determining what in fact is plausible. It assumes that the historical account relates to a historical reality, no matter how complex and indirect the process is by which the historian approximates this reality. Thus, although many historians have taken contemporary linguistic, semiotic, and literary theory seriously, they have in practice not accepted the idea that the texts with which they work have no reference to reality. To be sure every historical account is a construct, but a construct arising from a dialog between the historian and the past, one that does not occur in a vacuum but within a community of inquiring minds who share criteria of plausibility.

3. The End of Enlightenment?

The radical doubt in our century about the possibility of rational inquiry into history is, as we have suggested, closely tied to the growing discomfort with modern society and culture. This society has been considered the heir of the Enlightenment. Enlightenment was originally understood as the commitment to liberating human beings through rational reflection from arbitrary restraints, to permit every individual to develop his or her potentialities freely. In postmodernist discussion the Enlightenment has become the whipping boy responsible not only for emptying the world of meaning but also for creating the technological and administrative tools to dominate human beings. Postmodernist thought has built on a tradition of anti-Enlightenment sentiment that goes back to the antimodernism of eighteenth- and early nineteenth-century conservative and romantic thinkers. From here there is a line leading via Nietzsche and Heidegger to the radical right of the 1920s and 1930s.

Yet beginning in the 1940s, important aspects of this critique were appropriated by thinkers like Max Horkheimer, Theodor Adorno, and Herbert Marcuse, who applied Marxist concepts of alienation and commodification to a critique of modern culture. The Enlightenment, which had sought to free human beings by abolishing myth, they held, had created the new myth that scientific analysis could understand and through the technology it developed gain control over nature and man. Proceeding from a Marxist analysis they argued that behind the Enlightenment's proclamation of universal human rights lay concealed a hierarchical social, economic, and hence political order based on the rights of property. The great fault of the Enlightenment, they claimed, lay in its distorted view of reason, for which the ultimate aim is the reduction of truth to scientific, that is, quantitative formulations.[13] The belief in the omnipotence of this kind of science constituted a new myth. By abandoning concern for the qualitative aspects of existence, it lost sight of the critical perspective that constitutes the core of true science.

This characterization of the Enlightenment, later reiterated by Foucault, Derrida, and Lyotard, in my view represents a gross distortion. The Enlightenment admittedly had many conflicting aspects. To take Condorcet as one of its representatives, it sought to maximize wealth and well-being through the systematic application of scientific knowledge and the resulting technological knowhow to the realm of society.[14] But for Condorcet certainly science and technology were not ends in themselves but means for liberating men, and for him definitely also women, from the scourges of ignorance, deprivation, and tyranny. There was indeed a dual side to the Enlightenment: The universalism of the Enlightenment and its faith in rational planning and control, it has been argued, contained the seeds of the utopianism and totalitarianism of radicals from Robespierre to Lenin.[15] However, the stress on the autonomy of the enlightened individual presupposed determined opposition to all forms of arbitrary authority and total control.

The path from the Enlightenment to Auschwitz was infinitely more complex than Adorno or Foucault made it appear and was deeply indebted to the antimodernism of its opponents. The history of this century has taught us a great deal about the ambiguities of Enlightenment conceptions of human rights and rationality. Postmodernistist thought has made a substantial contribution to the contemporary historical discussions by its warnings against utopianism and conceptions of progress. This should lead us, however, not to abandonment and repudiation of the Enlightenment heritage but instead to a critical reexamination of it. This too has been the intent of a good deal of the new social and cultural history examined in this book. The alternative to an albeit chastened Enlightenment is barbarism.

Epilogue: A Retrospect at the Beginning of the Twenty-First Century

It has been seven years since this book first appeared in English and more than ten years since the original German edition was published.[1] The important changes in the world scene brought about by the end of the Cold War had by then been reflected only in small part in historical studies. In the last third of the twentieth century, the turn from an emphasis on the analytical social sciences to cultural factors continued, but with more diversified foci in the face of the rapidly changing world scene.

At the end of this book considerable attention was paid to the so-called postmodernist challenges to objective historical scholarship, but in recent years postmodernism has received less attention among historians.[2] In fact, the radical postmodern position was largely restricted to the United States—and, as we shall see, India—and to a lesser extent to Great Britain, although many of its intellectual roots derived from French poststructuralism. Its basic assumption—that language is a self-referential system that does not reflect but creates reality—denied the possibility of reconstructing the past as it was actually lived by human beings and abrogated the borderline between historical narratives and fiction. An extreme formulation of this radical position was voiced by Keith Jenkins in 1997, when he wrote that the whole modern conception of history (that is, that the historian can recapture the historical past), "now appears as a self-referential, problematical expression of interests, an ideological-interpretative discourse . . . In fact, history now appears to be just one more foundationless, positioned expression in a world of foundationless, positioned expressions."[3]

But this hardly corresponds to the assumptions with which historians operate, even today after the postmodernist challenge. The question of how one re-creates the past has become considerably more complex than it was either for the older political school or for social science–oriented historiography. The sheer objectivism of older historical scholarship has long been abandoned. As a matter of fact, it had never been unqualifiedly accepted by serious historians. Yet the awareness grew in recent years that historians approach their subject matter with questions and that the way to answer them is affected by the linguistic and conceptual tools with which historians construct their account.[4] But the radical form of postmodernist epistemological relativism has had little influence on historical study and historical writing. Nevertheless, ideas deriving from postmodernist thought and from the "linguistic turn" are reflected today in a great deal of historical writing, although these ideas originate not directly from postmodernism as such but from related developments in historical thought and practice.

Thus, indirectly, ideas similar to those of postmodernism continued to exert a profound influence on the reorientation of historical thought. This involves the questioning of history as a unilinear directional process leading to present day Western civilization. The radical consequence drawn from this redefinition of history— that history lacks all coherence—did not necessarily follow. Yet historians began to turn from constructing macrohistories to paying greater attention to smaller segments: to the lives and, significantly, to the experiences of little people. All this also had relevance for the way in which historians dealt with sources. The great impact here came less from postmodernist theories than from cultural anthropology,[5] linguistics, and semiotics, which all shared in the transformation of the intellectual climate in the last decades of the twentieth and the beginning of the twenty-first centuries. As we already saw, since the "linguistic turn" of the 1980s, attention increasingly was paid to the role of language in the form of discourse. Nevertheless, historians differed on the significance of language for historical inquiry.[6] While Joan Scott[7] argued that the texts with which the historian worked had no direct relation to an actual past—that language did not reflect but created reality—many more historians saw language and discourse as important tools for historical understanding yet also were aware that this linguistic turn occurred within specific socio-historical contexts.

At the same time, the conviction held by many social science–oriented historians, that political changes and events can best be explained in terms of social and economic factors, continued to lose credence. In the last ten years there have been two distinct new emphases in the treatment of political history.[8] The conception of what constitutes the political sphere broadened. Much political history, including that written by social science historians, still in the 1970s and 1980s focused on the state, generally the nation state, as the center of political activity domestically and internationally. This was true not only of historians in Europe and the English-speaking countries but also in China, Japan, and Korea, where national history had replaced dynastic history early in the twentieth century[9] and in the states in Asia and Africa that became independent after 1945. Yet even in the former colonial states, the idea of the nation state has been challenged in recent years, most importantly in India, where since the 1980s historians of the group around the *Subaltern Studies*[10] have emphasized not only that the Western idea of the nation state is elitist but that it is inapplicable to older Indian history with its social and cultural diversities. But new foci appeared—particularly in the United States—which placed greater emphasis on social, ethnic, and gender-related factors. The nation was now less frequently seen as an organic unit with a unified sense of identity but rather as a conglomerate of subordinate identifiable units. The exhibit of the National Museum of History in Washington, D.C., in the 1990s reflected the notion of a multi-ethnic nation with different traditions, yet it is this multiculturalism that is reshaping American identity without dissolving it.

Moreover, the concept of class—still popular in social history—underwent change. E. P. Thompson in *Making of the English Working Class* (1963) understood class no longer solely in socio-economic terms but as also involving outlooks and patterns of thought—in brief, aspects of culture. But this view with roots in Marxism, even if now Cultural Marxism, which still saw class as an integrative and integrating unit, seems outdated today, because it fails to take into account the much more complex character of societies. Ethnicity, gender, religion, and ideologies, among other factors, have assumed much greater importance in the analysis of politics and societies. At times this has led to an isolation of cultural history, neglecting the larger configuration of economic and political factors.

Moreover the concept of what constitutes not just the political, but also the social, sphere has broadened in two ways. One, which we have just mentioned, is the extension of the political and social spheres to encompass the diverse elements of culture; the other entails understanding the private sphere in terms of power relations that involve aspects of everyday life. Michel Foucault had already prepared the ground for understanding how power relations operate on the interpersonal level. While the exercise of power previously had been seen in terms of such powerful central institutions as government or the economy, the extragovernmental forms in which power operates and permeates all aspects of life received greater attention. Again the danger remains that the socio-political and economic contexts of culture are neglected.

And this brings us to recent feminist history, in which the broadened conception of power plays a central role. A key idea of feminist history was the subjugation of women. Earlier feminist history had been accused of being "too white, too middle class, and too heterosexual."[11] Feminist history increasingly gave way in the 1990s to "gender" studies, that is, the relation of women and men in a historical and social context. Here questions of economic status, ethnicity, sexual orientation, legislation, mores, and customs were addressed. Postmodernist ideas played a greater role in feminist theory than in other areas of historical thought. For some feminist theorists, like Joan Scott, patterns of patriarchal domination were deeply embedded in traditional language and in the "logocentric" tradition of Western philosophy since classical antiquity, thereby calling for the deconstruction of all historical, political, and philosophic texts of the West. On more empirical grounds, feminist scholars studied the means by which women and other subordinated or marginalized groups sought to affect the status quo and also reexamined from a new feminist perspective such crucial aspects of history as the emergence of capitalism, the French Revolution, slavery and emancipation, social reform in North America and Europe, civil rights, and national liberation movements in the colonial world.[12] Increasingly since the mid-1980s, examinations of the differences among women have supplemented those between men and women. But an important development of the last fifteen years has been that women's history and gender history have been increasingly integrated into general history.

Another area that was affected by ideas parallel to postmodernism without fully sharing its epistemological relativism concerns the central role of memory.[13] A great deal of the reconstruction of historical memory relies on oral history. Oral history was well established by the 1980s. As early as the 1930s, a major publicly funded project in the United States interrogated the few surviving former slaves. As mentioned earlier in the book, an extensive German oral history project in the 1980s explored how common people, particularly industrial workers, experienced the Third Reich. In the final days of the Soviet Union the Memorial oral history group sought through individual interviews to reconstruct life under Stalinism. By the 1990s, not only the experiences of victims of the Nazi Holocaust but also testimony by perpetrators were extensively studied.[14] Although aware of the unreliability of oral testimony, the purpose of these interviews was still to gain a better understanding of a real past. A second, very different, approach to historical memory was initiated by the French editors of the collection *Lieux de Mémoire* (Places of Memory).[15] The editors proposed an alternative to established academic history, which sought to reestablish the past on the basis of documentary evidence, and instead focused on history as it was remembered collectively. Instead of individual memories, it relied on such tangible reminders as monuments, national holidays, and sacred places that shaped collective identity. For the editors of *Lieux de Mémoire* this was national identity and specifically a French identity. A major project at the German Historical Museum in Berlin explored how European peoples as well as those in the United States and Israel remembered their past, studying the key roles that legends and myths played in the invention of national identities.[16]

While on the one hand historical writing tended more often to turn from macro to microthemes and from large processes and structures to the small and local, the condition of the contemporary world made inescapable large-scale investigations of the transformations that present-day societies are undergoing. Two very different syntheses resulted from the changed conditions after the collapse of the Soviet Union. We have already briefly mentioned Francis Fukuyama's *The End of History,* published in 1992. "All countries undergoing economic modernization," he argued, "must increasingly resemble each other." This leads Fukuyama to the question of "Whether at the end of the twentieth century, it makes sense for us once again to speak of a coherent and directional History of mankind that will eventually lead the major part of mankind to liberal democracy," a question that he answers in the affirmative. The driving motor for this development is for him the capitalist market economy; the model that heralds the future is the United States. Fukuyama was confident that a world made up of liberal democracies would have little incentive to wage war.[17]

This conception turned out to be an illusion, as the events after the end of the Cold War soon showed. It rested on a very simplistic model of modernization[18] that must have appeared inadequate to many social and political historians who, even before 1989, already were very much aware of the role of culture and of cultural divisions. It also operated with a conception of liberal, capitalist democracies as harmonious societies that failed to take into consideration the role of social inequality and conflict among various interest groups, be they economic, ideological, religious, gender, or ethnic. And it set Western conditions as the norm for non-Western societies.

Samuel Huntington, in *The Clash of Civilizations* (1996), presented a countermodel that stressed the role of culture, while de-emphasizing economic and social factors. "In the post–Cold War world," he wrote, "the most important distinctions among people are not ideological, political, or economic. They are cultural."[19] Like Spengler and Toynbee earlier in the last century, he identifies a number of civilizations as the decisive units on the world scene and foresees continuing conflicts among these civilizations, especially among the West, the Islamic world, and China. But he sees these cultures in essentialist terms, as organic units in which transformations in time and internal divisions did not play a major role. Jettisoning all hopes for international peace and coexistence, he argues: "The survival of the West depends on Americans reaffirming their Western identity and Westerners accepting their civilization as unique and not universal, and uniting to renew and preserve it against challenges from non-Western societies."[20] For him this also means that the multiculturalism endorsed by many social and cultural historians today represents a cancer that threatens to destroy the West.

Neither Fukuyama's nor Huntington's model has been taken seriously in recent historiography, not only because of the political implications of their work but also because they operate on a speculative plane of global history alien to historians who avoid such schemes in their empirical work. However, the developments of the past decade and a half have shown that neither the turn to microhistory nor the older patterns of national and regional history are sufficient for dealing with the transformations that are taking place on a global scale. It is important to reexamine the character of modernization. With the cultural turn in historical thought since the 1970s, the very notion of modernization went out of fashion. Modernization assumed the progressive replacement of "traditional" by "modern" outlooks, institutions, and behavior. The driving forces were intellectual, scientific, technological, and, most important, economic. Its roots were in Western culture, but its scope was universal. It assumed the interrelatedness among "the emergence of capitalism, industrialization, the rise of liberal democratic structures, the building of the nation state, the emergence of pluralist society and social relations built on achievement, the advancement of science, certain personality structures, certain belief systems, and [various] states of mind."[21] The idea of modernization was rejected on two grounds, first of all because of its macrohistorical character. It imposed a master narrative on history, but history, as its critics argued, was not a coherent, directional process. Second, it was rejected because it viewed the development of history as normative and desirable, desirable not only for the West but for the world generally. It overlooked the negative sides of progress and modernization, the great catastrophes of the twentieth century: world wars, genocide, and fascist and Communist dictatorships. For many of its critics it was closely connected with Western imperialism in its colonial and post-colonial forms, involving the political, economic, and cultural domination of the non-West. The critique of modernization and Western modernity with its supposed roots in the Enlightenment offered by some Indian intellectuals in recent years also took a form similar to that put forward by postmodernist thinkers in the West.[22]

Yet it is indisputable that there are processes of modernization taking place before our eyes, most clearly in the scientific, technological, and, of course, economic spheres, and that in these areas modernization, although largely Western in origin, has transformed societies globally. Thus modernization must be taken seriously on a world scale. The older models of modernization are obviously insufficient when applied to non-Western societies, and in previous chapters we saw that these models also proved to be inadequate for the analysis of developments in the West. As we saw earlier in this book, German historians in the 1960s and 1970s sought to explain why the course of German history in the nineteenth and the first half of the twentieth centuries deviated from what they considered the normal process of modernization as represented by Great Britain or the United States, in which industrialization was accompanied by democratization.[23] Recent studies have shown not only that there were differing paths of modernization in Europe—German National Socialism, Italian Fascism, and Soviet Communism also represented forms of modernization[24]—but that the much-praised English model did not reflect the complexities and contradictions of modern English, French, or American history.[25]

Applied to the non-Western world this model has proved to be even more inadequate. Considerable modernization has occurred as part of the globalization of corporate capitalism, with similar developments in the technological and economic spheres and—to an extent, differing in different societies—also in consumer patterns and popular culture. There are thus elements of homogenization that are nowhere complete. Various societies have *adapted* aspects of Western modernity without fully *adopting* them, fitting them into the indigenous culture. In a recent series of essays, *Provincializing Europe,* a distinguished Indian social scientist, Dipesh Chakrabarty, sought to demonstrate the parochialism of a Western view of historical development in terms of stages toward modernity for which the colonial cultures represented archaic or premodern forms destined to give way in the process of modernization. However, he acknowledged that Western forms of science and social scientific rationality had generally been adopted in the formally colonized world, particularly in South Asia. He notes "that today the so-called European intellectual tradition is the only one alive in the social science departments of most, if not all, [Indian] universities." Thus few if any Indian social scientists would base their theories on older Indian thinkers. One result of European colonial rule in India has been "that the intellectual traditions once unbroken and alive in Sanskrit or Persian or Arabic are now 'truly dead.' "[26] But on the political and cultural level, the patterns introduced by the colonizers are by no means unchallenged. On one hand the anticolonial and postcolonial movements were deeply influenced by Enlightenment notions of human rights and democracy. On the other hand, they coexisted with older ideas of social organization and politics in which ancient Hindu religious beliefs that would be considered superstitious today and incompatible with Indian democracy persisted. And these beliefs were by no means premodern but constituted an important form of modernity. There is thus not one modernity but various modernities; historians and sociologists have begun to speak of "multiple modernities."[27] Indian modernity according to Chakrabarty cannot be understood without referring to its religious roots. But, as he points out, modernity, which one might think posits a secular outlook, is challenged by Pentacostal revivals in the United States as well as in Latin America, and also in radical forms of Orthodox Judaism, Islam, and Hinduism that rest not solely on indigenous traditions but also on their very antimodernist use of modern means to mobilize a mass following.

The study of modernities by necessity leads to comparative global studies. The years since 1990 have seen an increasing expansion of historical studies beyond national and Western themes. Yet at this point there have been many discussions of the desirability of global historical studies and of the methodologies required but little actual work. The professional historians have been at a disadvantage compared to historical sociologists. Particularly in Europe, historians have concentrated until now on their national histories; in the United States since World War II relatively more historians have become specialists in non-Western fields, but generally with an expertise on a particular region. Historians also have been trained to rely on archives and primary materials, which tended to tie them to national or local history. In contrast, many sociologists, economists, and even political scientists viewed their science in nomothetic, macrohistorical terms, seeking generalizations. Historians today increasingly turn to comparative intercultural studies. There are more specialists today than there were ten years ago in East Asian, South Asian, Islamic, sub-Saharan, and even Oceanic history. The studies of these areas have moved closer to the methodologies of the social sciences, but in many cases they are not yet comparative and intercultural. There is now a *Journal of World History*, founded in 1990, and a *Journal of Global History* is in the planning stages. Older studies of global history such as Immanuel Wallerstein's *The Modern World System* (1978–89) focused on the penetration of the non-Western world by European capitalism, with little concern for cultural aspects, thus following modernization theory, although from a critical Marxist perspective.

The need for global history is obvious today,[28] yet a large number of conceptual and methodological problems still need to be solved. Given the complexities of societies and culture, comparative studies—and this is even more the case when comparisons operate on an intercultural, global plane—require clear definitions of what is to be compared and by what methods. In this sense the Weberian conception of "ideal types" is not outdated. But we are aware today that globalization, driven by market forces, has not resulted in homogenization on cultural, social, political, or even economic planes but rather in diversifications rooted in indigenous traditions. Aware of the complexities of intercultural and intersocietal comparisons, and also realizing that globalization is not a one-way process by which the patterns of the highly developed capitalist countries are transferred abroad, historians and social scientists engaged in comparative studies have in the last few years begun to speak of "entangled histories."[29] It is also evident that global studies cannot be carried out by individual historians in isolation but instead require the coordinated cooperation of researchers in various fields as well as interdisciplinary methodologies that integrate historical inquiry with the social and cultural sciences and the humanities. At this point we are still very much at the beginning of such coordinated projects.

So far in this book we have dealt primarily with Western historiography. In part this dates its first edition. There is, however, some justification for this approach. The flow of historical, or for that matter social-scientific, work has until now been largely in one direction, from Western countries outward. Since the late nineteenth century, a tremendous number of Western works have been translated into Japanese, Chinese, Korean, and, to a lesser extent, Arabic and Farsi, but very little has flowed in the opposite direction. India is the exception, but largely only in the last three decades since the foundation of the *Subaltern Studies.* One reason for this is that since the mid-nineteenth century English has been in wide use in India as the academic language. Indian secondary and tertiary education was patterned on the British model, and not only were many Indian intellectuals trained in Great Britain, but in recent years a number of Indian scholars have held prestigious positions at American and British universities. It is particularly with the postmodernist critique of Western modernity that Indian writers have participated in the Western discourse. At the core of the Indian critique of Western modernity is, of course, the trauma of colonialism. The *Subaltern Studies* criticized the established Indian anticolonial historiography, which had followed established patterns of narrative political history, as inapplicable to the Indian past and because, with its focus on the leading political and social elites, it neglected the subaltern classes. Thus these scholars turned to a "history from below" at the same time as their Western colleagues. Yet (again like their colleagues in the West) they were divided in their assessment of the Enlightenment roots of modern Western culture. Ashis Nandy saw the entire modern tradition of scientific thinking as a vast disservice committed to establishing colonial and later postcolonial hegemony over the non-Western world. He condemned "the links the idea of history has established with the modern nation-state, the secular worldview, the Baconian concept of scientific rationality, nineteenth-century theories of progress, and, in recent decades, development . . . complicit with many forms of violence, exploitation." This world view replaced those of cultures that depended on "myths, legends, and epics" to define themselves. Nandy calls not for an alternative history but for the negation of history.[30] On the other hand, Sumit Sarkar, a leading Indian social historian who was once associated with *Subaltern Studies,* warned his countrymen against uncritically accepting Edward Said's focus on "colonial discourses, through which Enlightenment rationalism supposedly established cultural domination," a postmodern analysis that according to Sarkar "runs the danger of ignoring precisely the things that make modern Western arrogance so excessively oppressive: its linkage with very material forms of imperialist economic and political power." For him Nandy's romantic idealization of a harmonious premodern past overlooks the inequalities and oppressions in traditional Indian society. Instead, he argues, "a selective appropriation of Western discourses of liberal rights could often be helpful, as indeed it has been on the whole with respect also to issues of caste inequality, gender justice and class oppression." While recognizing the positive effects in postmodern and postcolonial deconstruction in laying bare the power relations inherent in modern discourses, he warns against the linguistic-cum-literary turn's inversion of the traditional primacy of logic over rhetoric.[31]

A final word about recent histories of historiography. Many of the works have followed traditional lines little affected by the literary turn which Hayden White introduced with *Metahistory* in 1973. A number of books on the history of historical writing appeared in the 1990s in Western languages, yet all of them, including this book, dealt only with European and North American authors.[32] There was no comparative intercultural examination of historical thought. A number of collections of essays have appeared that dealt with approaches to history in individual cultures, important stepping-stones to a broadly comparative approach.[33] But this comprehensive perception is still lacking. The problems we have mentioned that make it difficult to write global history also confront an intercultural, comparative study of historiography. Such a history is still a project for the future.[34]

Notes

Introduction (pp. 1–19)

1. Georg G. Iggers, *New Directions in European Historiography* (Middletown, Conn., 1975, 1984).

2. See Leopold von Ranke, "Preface to the First Edition of *Histories of the Latin and Germanic Nations*," in Leopold von Ranke, *Theory and Practice of History*, ed. Georg G. Iggers and Konrad von Moltke (Indianapolis, 1973), 137.

3. See Hayden White, *Metahistory: The Historical Imagination in Nineteenth-Century Europe* (Baltimore, 1973); *The Tropics of Discourse. Essays in Cultural Criticism* (Baltimore, 1982); *The Content of the Form: Narrative Discourse and Historical Representation* (Baltimore, 1987).

4. See Leopold von Ranke, "On the Character of Historical Science," in *The Theory and Practice of History*, 33–46; and "The Great Powers," ibid., 100.

5. See William Keylor, *Academy and Community: The Foundation of the French Historical Profession* (Cambridge, Mass., 1975).

6. See John Higham, *History: Professional Scholarship in America* (Baltimore, 1983); Peter Novick, *That Noble Dream: The "Objectivity Question" and the American Historical Profession* (Cambridge, 1988).

7. See, for example, the section "Historical Science," in *Congress of the Arts and Sciences: Universal Exposition, St. Louis, 1904*, vol. 2 (Boston, 1906).

8. See Bryce Lyon, *Henri Pirenne: A Biographical and Intellectual Study* (Ghent, 1974).

9. See Burckhardt's *Reflections on History* (Indianapolis, 1979) and *Briefe*, 10 vols. (Basel, 1949–86).

10. E.g., Friedrich Nietzsche, "On the Uses and Disadvantages of History for Life," in his *Untimely Meditations* (Cambridge, 1983). See also Allan Megill, *Prophets of Extremity: Nietzsche, Heidegger, Foucault, Derrida* (Berkeley, 1985).

11. Erik Wolf, *Europe and the People Without History* (Berkeley, 1982).

12. John Higham, "Beyond Consensus: The Historian as Moral Critic," *American Historical Review* 57 (1961–62), 609–25.

13. Michael Harrington, *The Other America: Poverty in the United States* (Baltimore, 1962).

14. See Daniel Boorstin, *The Genius of American Politics* (Chicago, 1953).

15. Daniel Bell, *The End of Ideology: On the Exhaustion of Political Ideas in the Fifties* (New York, 1960).

16. See Allan Megill, "'Grand Narratives' and the Discipline of History," in Frank Ankersmit and Hans Kellner, eds., *A New Philosophy of History* (Chicago, 1995), 151–73.

17. Oswald Spengler, *The Decline of the West*, 2 vols. (New York, 1926).

18. Marc Bloch, *La Société féodale*, 2 vols. (Paris, 1939–40), English: *Feudal Society* (Chicago, 1964); Fernand Braudel, *La Méditerranée et le monde méditerranéen à l'époque de Phillippe II* (Paris, 1949), 2d enlarged ed., 2 vols. (Paris, 1966), English: *The Mediterranean and the Mediterranean World in the Age of Philip II*, 2 vols. (New York, 1972–74).

19. E.g., *The Civilization of the Renaissance in Italy* (New York, 1945).

20. See Braudel, *The Mediterranean and the Mediterranean*.

21. See Jacques Le Goff, *Time, Work and Culture in the Middle Ages* (Chicago, 1980).

22. Edward P. Thompson, "Time, Work-Discipline and Industrial Capitalism," *Past and Present* 38 (1967), 56–97.

23. Claude Lévi-Strauss, *Savage Mind* (Chicago, 1968).

24. See Robert Fogel and Geoffrey Elton, *Two Ways to the Past? Two Views of History* (New Haven, 1983).

25. See Megill, *Prophets of Extremity*.

26. See chapter 10.

27. See Art Berman, *From the New Criticism to Deconstruction: The Reception of Structuralism and Post-Structuralism* (Urbana, 1988).

28. Fernand de Saussure, *Course in General Linguistics* (London, 1983).

29. See Roland Barthes, "The Discourse of History," trans. Stephen Bann, in *Comparative Criticism: A Yearbook*, vol. 3 (1981), 3–28.

30. See above, n. 3.

31. Jacques Derrida, *Of Grammatology* (Baltimore, 1976), 158.

32. Clifford Geertz, *The Interpretation of Cultures* (New York, 1973).

33. See Lionel Gossman, "History and Literature: Reproduction or Signification," in Robert H. Canary and Henry Kozicki, eds., *The Writing of History: Literary Form and Historical Understanding* (Madison, 1978), 32–33.

34. Hayden White, "The Historical Text as Literary Artifact," in *The Tropics of Discourse*, 82.

35. Hans Kellner, "The Politics of Interpretation," in W. J. T. Mitchell, ed., *The Politics of Interpretation* (Chicago, 1982), 301.
36. Robert Berkhofer, "The Challenge of Poetics to (Normal) Historical Practice," *Poetics Today* 9 (1988), 435–52. Berkhofer is by no means totally critical here of historical realism.
37. See the excellent recent review essay by John H. Zammito, "Are We Being Theoretical Yet? The New Historicism, The New Philosophy of History, and 'Practicing Historians,'" *The Journal of Modern History* 65 (1993), 783–814; and Jan R. Veenstra, "The New Historicism of Stephen Greenblatt: On Poetics of Culture and the Interpretation of Shakespeare," *History and Theory* 34 (1995), 174–98. See also H. Aram Veeser, ed., *The New Historicism* (New York, 1989).
38. See Stephen Greenblatt, *Renaissance Self-Fashioning: From More to Shakespeare* (Chicago, 1980); *Shakespearean Negotiations: The Circulation of Social Energy in Elizabethan England* (Oxford, 1988); ed., *The Power of Forms in the English Renaissance* (Norman, Okla., 1982).
39. See Stephen Greenblatt, *Marvellous Possessions: The Wonder of the New World* (Chicago, 1991).
40. Stephen Greenblatt, "Towards a Poetics of Culture," in his *Learning to Curse: Essays in Early Modern Culture* (New York, 1990).
41. F. A. Ankersmit, "History and Postmodernism," *History and Theory* 28 (1989), 137–53, reprinted in Ankersmit, *History and Tropology* (Berkeley, 1994); also Ankersmit, "Historicism: An Attempt at Synthesis," *History and Theory* 34 (1995), 143–61, Georg G. Iggers's "Comments," in ibid., 162–67, and Ankersmit's reply, in ibid., 168–73.
42. See Kellner's yet unpublished presentation in the session "Fictionality, Narrativity, Objectivity" at the International Congress of Historical Sciences in Montreal August 27–September 3, 1995; see also Kellner, *Language and Historical Representation: Getting the Language Crooked* (Madison, 1989); coeditor with F. R. Ankersmit, *A New Philosophy of History* (Chicago, 1995).
43. See the *Actes/Proceedings* of the 18th International Congress of Historical Sciences (Montreal, 1995), 159–82.
44. Roger Chartier, ibid., 174.
45. Ibid.
46. Zammito, "Are We Being Theoretical Yet?," 804.
47. See Max Horkheimer and Theodor W. Adorno, *Dialectic of Enlightenment* (New York, 1975).
48. See Megill, *Prophets of Extremity*.

49. See Joan Scott, *Gender and the Politics of History* (New York, 1988).
50. See Saul Friedlaender, ed., *Probing the Limits of Representation: Nazism and the Final Solution* (Cambridge, Mass., 1992).
51. Hayden White, "Historical Emplotment and the Problem of Truth," in ibid., 37–53.
52. Clifford Geertz, "Thick Description: Toward an Interpretive Theory of Culture," in his *The Interpretation of Cultures: Selected Essays* (New York, 1973), 5; see also his definition of culture in "Religion as a Cultural System" in ibid., 89: "the culture concept to which I adhere has neither multiple referents nor, as I can see, any unusual ambiguity: it denotes an historically transmitted pattern of meanings embodied in symbols, a system of inherited conceptions expressed in symbolic forms by means of which men communicate, perpetuate, and develop their knowledge about and attitudes toward life."
53. On the History Workshop movement, see below, pp. 89–94.
54. Georges Lefebvre, *The French Revolution*, 2 vols. (New York, 1970); also his *The Coming of the French Revolution* (Princeton, 1989).
55. Albert Soboul, *The French Revolution 1787–1799* (London, 1989); also his *The Parisian Sans Culottes and the French Revolution* (Westport, 1979).
56. Alfred Cobban, *The Social Interpretation of the French Revolution* (Cambridge, 1968).
57. François Furet, *Interpreting the French Revolution* (Cambridge, 1981); also Furet and Mona Ozouf, eds., *The Transformation of Political Culture*, 3 vols. (Oxford, 1989).
58. Lynn Hunt, *Politics, Culture, and Class in the French Revolution* (Berkeley, 1986).
59. William Sewell, *Work and Revolution in France, The Language of Labor from the Old Regime to 1848* (Cambridge, 1980).
60. Simon Schama, *Citizens* (New York, 1990).
61. See E. G. Fukuyama, "The End of History?," *The National Interest* 9 (Summer 1989), 3–18; see also his *The End of History and the Last Man* (New York, 1992).
62. Thomas Kuhn, *The Structure of Scientific Revolutions*, 2d ed. (Chicago, 1970).

1. Classical Historicism as a Model for Historical Scholarship (pp. 23–30)

1. *Bildung* is a term that cannot easily be translated and has to be seen within the framework of German intellectual culture. Neither of the

common translations as "culture" or "education" suffice. Fritz Ringer attempts a definition: "the vision of learning as personal self-fulfillment through interpretive interaction with venerated texts." "The essentially interpretive model of *Bildung* inspired the dominant hermeneutic tradition in German philological and historical scholarship, as well as the German conception of the *Geisteswissenschaften*. . . . The objective of *Bildung* implied personal and evaluative insight *(Weltanschauung)*, rather than manipulative intervention in nature or in social processes." Ringer, *Fields of Knowledge: French Academic Culture in Comparative Perspective, 1890–1920* (Cambridge, 1992), 2.

2. Fritz Ringer, *The Decline of the German Mandarins: The German Academic Community, 1890–1933* (Cambridge, Mass., 1969).

3. *Geschichten der romanischen und germanischen Völker von 1494 bis 1514* (Leipzig, 1824), English: *History of the Latin and Teutonic Nations* (London, 1887).

4. *Zur Kritik neuerer Geschichtschreiber*, published separately that same year.

5. Cf. "Preface to the First Edition of *Histories of the Latin and Germanic Nations*," in Leopold von Ranke, *The Theory and Practice of History*, ed. Georg G. Iggers and Konrad von Moltke (Indianapolis, 1973), 137.

6. "On the Character of Historical Science," in ibid., 38.

7. In ibid., 41.

8. "The Great Powers," in ibid., 100.

9. "A Dialogue on Politics," in ibid., 119.

10. See Ranke, "Über die Verwandtschaft und den Unterschied der Historie und der Politik," *Sämtliche Werke*, vol. 24, 280–93.

11. Lord Acton, "German Schools of History," *English Historical Review* 1 (1986), 7–42.

12. Herbert B. Adams used this expression in "New Methods of Study in History," in Johns Hopkins University, *Studies in History and Political Science* II (1884), 65; see also Adams, "Leopold von Ranke," American Historical Association *Papers*, III (1888), 104–5.

13. On recruitment of historians in Germany, see Wolfgang Weber, *Priester der Klio: Historisch-sozialwissenschaftliche Studien zur Herkunft und Karriere deutscher Historiker und zur Geschichte der Geschichtswissenschaft 1800–1970* (Frankfurt am Main, 1984); comparatively Christian Simon, *Staat und Gesellschaft in Frankreich und Deutschland 1871–1914: Situation und Werk von Geschichtsprofessoren an den Universitäten Berlin, München, Paris*, 2 vols. (Bern, 1988).

14. See William Keylor, *Academy and Community: The Foundation of the French Historical Profession* (Cambridge, Mass., 1975).

15. See Georg G. Iggers, "Historicism: The History and the Meaning of the Term," *Journal of the History of Ideas* 56 (1995), 129–51. I am consciously avoiding the term "historicism" because it has too many often contradictory meanings. I would have preferred the term "historism" (*Historismus*)), which more closely designates the world outloook and the scholarly practice of the nineteenth- and first half of the twentieth-century German historians whom we have discussed in this volume. But the term "historism" virtually disappeared from English after Croce's writings became well known with their translation in the 1920s and 30s. Croce spoke of *storicismo* in contrast to the older term *istorismo*, which corresponded more closely to the German uses.

16. Ortega y Gasset, *History as a System and Other Essays Toward a Philosophy of History* (New York, 1941), 217.

17. Friedrich Meinecke, *Die Entstehung des Historismus, Werke* III (München, 1965), 4, English: *Historism: The Rise of a New Historical Outlook* (New York, 1972).

18. Herbert Adams, "Leopold von Ranke," 104–5. See also Georg G. Iggers, "The Image of Ranke in American and German Historical Thought," *History and Theory* 2 (1962), 17–40; also Novick, *That Noble Dream.*

19. Leopold von Ranke, "On Progress in History," in *The Theory and Practice of History*, 53.

20. Leopold von Ranke, "On the Character of Historical Science," in ibid., 46.

21. Ernst Troeltsch, "Die Krisis des Historismus," *Die Neue Rundschau* 33 (1922), I, 572–90; *Der Historismus und seine Probleme, Gesammelte Schriften* (Aalen, 1961), vol. 4.

22. See Karl Heussi, *Die Krisis des Historismus* (Tübingen, 1932), and Karl Mannheim, "Historismus," in Kurt H. Wolf, ed., *Wissenssoziologie: Auswahl aus dem Werk* (Neuwied, 1970).

2. The Crisis of Classical Historicism (pp. 31–35)

1. Karl Lamprecht, *Deutsche Geschichte*, 12 vols. (Berlin, 1891–1909). The best critical examination of the Lamprecht controversy and of Lamprecht the man, scholar, and political figure is Roger Chickering, *Karl Lamprecht: A German Academic Life (1856–1915)* (Atlantic Highlands, N.J., 1993).

2. See Karl Lamprecht, *Alte und neue Richtungen in der Geschichtswissenschaft* (Berlin, 1896).
3. Cited in Susan D. Schultz, "History as a Moral Force Against Individualism: Karl Lamprecht and the Methodological Controversies in the German Human Sciences," Ph.D. dissertation, University of Chicago, 1984, 282.
4. On the political context, see Chickering, *Karl Lamprecht*.
5. Dietrich Schäfer, "Das eigentliche Arbeitsgebiet der Geschichte," in *Aufsätze, Vorträge und Reden*, vol. 1 (Jena, 1913), 264–90.
6. Eberhard Gothein, *Die Aufgabe der Kulturgeschichte* (Leipzig, 1889).
7. On Lamprecht's supposed materialism see Felix Rachfahl, "Deutsche Geschichte vom wirtschaftlichen Standpunkt," *Preußische Jahrbücher* 83 (1895), 48–96; also Georg von Below, "Die neue historische Methode," *Historische Zeitschrift* 81 (1896), 265; on the question of whether he is a Marxist, see ibid., 265–66.
8. On the interest in social history on the eve of the Lamprecht controversy, see Gerhard Oestreich, "Die Fachhistorie und die Anfänge der sozialgeschichtlichen Forschung in Deutschland," *Historische Zeitschrift* 208 (1969), 320–63.
9. Emile Durkheim, "Cours de science sociale, leçon d'ouverture," *Revue internationale de l'enseignement* 15 (1888), 23–48; see also his *The Rules of Sociological Method* (New York, 1938).
10. François Simiand, "Méthode historique et sciences sociales," *Revue de Synthèse Historique* 6 (1903), 1–22.
11. See Richard Hofstadter, *The Progressive Historians: Turner, Beard, Parrington* (New York, 1968); and Ernst Breisach, *American Progressive History: An Experiment in Modernization* (Chicago, 1993).
12. See the section "Historical Science," at which Woodrow Wilson, Frederick Jackson Turner, William Milligan Sloane, James Harvey Robinson, J. B. Bury, and Karl Lamprecht presented papers, in *Congress of Arts and Sciences: Universal Exposition, St. Louis, 1904*, vol. 2 (Boston, 1906). Max Weber, Ernst Troeltsch, and Adolf Harnack were present in St. Louis and presented papers at other sections.

3. Economic and Social History in Germany and the Beginnings of Historical Sociology (pp. 36–40)

1. Karl Lamprecht, *Deutsches Wirtschaftsleben im Mittelalter: Untersuchungen über die Entwicklung der materiellen Kultur des platten*

Landes auf Grund der Quellen zunächst des Mosellandes, 3 vols. (Leipzig, 1885–86).

2. On Dilthey, see the most recent work, Jacob Owensby, *Dilthey and the Narrative of History* (Ithaca, 1994).

3. Otto Hintze, "Über individualistische und kollektivistische Geschichtsauffassung," *Historische Zeitschrift* 78 (1897), 60–67.

4. Max Weber, "Roscher und Knies und die logischen Probleme der historischen Nationalökonomie," in *Gesammelte Aufsätze zur Wissenschaftslehre* (Tübingen, 1968), 1–145.

5. Otto Hintze, "Wesen und Verbreitung des Feudalismus," in *Staat und Verfassung* (Göttingen, 1962), 84–119; "Der moderne Kapitalismus als historisches Individuum," in *Soziologie und Geschichte* (Göttingen, 1964), 374–426. A version of the essay on capitalism and the essay on individualistic and collectivistic approaches to history, which he contributed to the Lamprecht controversy, are included in an English collection of his writings, *The Historical Essays of Otto Hintze* (Oxford, 1975).

6. Max Weber, "Die 'Objektivität' sozialwissenschaftlicher und sozialpolitischer Erkenntnis," in *Gesammelte Aufsätze zur Wissenschaftslehre*, 155. Translated as "'Objectivity' in Social Science and Social Policy," in *Max Weber on the Methodology of the Social Sciences*, trans. and ed. Edward Shils and Henry A. Finch (Glencoe, Ill., 1949), 58.

4. American Traditions of Social History (pp. 41–47)

1. See Adam Ferguson, *Essay on the History of Civil Society* (Edinburgh, 1767).

2. Frederick Jackson Turner, "The Significance of the Frontier in American History," reprinted in Turner, *The Frontier in American History* (New York, 1920), 1–38.

3. Bryce Lyon, *Henri Pirenne. A Biographical and Intellectual Study*, (Ghent, 1974).

4. John Higham, "Beyond Consensus: The Historian as Moral Critic," *American Historical Review* 67 (1961–62), 609–25.

5. Daniel Bell, *The End of Ideology: On the Exhaustion of Political Ideas in the Fifties* (New York, 1960).

6. Emmanuel Le Roy Ladurie, *The Territory of the Historian* (Chicago, 1979), 15.

7. Geoffrey Barraclough, *Main Trends in History* (New York, 1979), 89.

8. Robert Fogel and Douglass North, *Railroads and American Economic Growth* (Baltimore, 1964).
9. Walt Rostow, *Stages of Economic Growth: A Non-Communist Manifesto* (Cambridge, 1960).
10. Karl Marx, "Preface" to *Capital*, vol. 1 (New York, 1977).
11. Alexander Gerschenkron, *Economic Backwardness in Historical Perspective* (Cambridge, Mass., 1962).
12. Robert Fogel and Stanley Engerman, *Time on the Cross*, 2 vols. (New York, 1974).
13. See Herbert Gutman, *Slavery and the Numbers Game: A Critique of Time on the Cross* (Urbana, 1975).
14. See Robert Fogel and Geoffrey Elton, *Which Road to the Past? Two Views of History* (New York, 1983).

5. France: The Annales (pp. 51–64)

1. On the history of the *Annales*, see Peter Burke, *The French Historical Revolution. The Annales School 1929–89* (Stanford, 1990); also Troian Stoianovich, *French Historical Method: The Annales Paradigm* (Ithaca, 1976).
2. On Bloch, see the biography by Carol Fink, *Marc Bloch* (Cambridge, 1989); most recently Ulrich Raulff, *Ein Historiker im 20. Jahrhundert: Marc Bloch* (Frankfurt am Main, 1995).
3. See Lutz Raphael, "Historikerkontroversen im Spannungsfeld zwischen Berufshabitus, Fächerkonkurrenz und sozialen Deutungsmustern, Lamprecht-Streit und französischer Methodenstreit der Jahrhundertwende in vergleichender Perspektive," *Historische Zeitschrift* 251 (1990), 352.
4. François Simiand, "Méthode historique et sciences sociales," *Revue de Synthèse Historique* 6 (1903), 1–22.
5. Marc Bloch, *Les Rois thaumaturges* (Paris, 1924), English: *The Royal Touch* (London, 1973).
6. Lucien Febvre, *Martin Luther: A Destiny* (London, 1930).
7. In a letter to the Dutch historian Johan Huizinga of October 2, 1933, Lucien Febvre explained that the *Annales* have taken the place of the *Vierteljahrschrift*, which has become an almost exclusively German journal with a very different understanding of social history than that of the *Annales*. See Jan Huizinga, *Briefwisseling*, vol. 2 (Utrecht, 1990), 484.
8. The most recent book on Droysen in English is Robert Southard, *Droysen and the Prussian School of History* (Lexington, Kentucky,

1995), which, however, is primarily concerned with the political relevance of Droysen's thought. His historical theory is best discussed in Jörn Rüsen, *Begriffene Geschichte: Genesis und Begründung der Geschichtstheorie J. G. Droysens* (Paderborn, 1969).

9. Marc Bloch, *The Historian's Craft* (New York, 1953). The French title is *Apologie pour l'histoire: Le métier de l'historien* (Paris, 1949), posthumously published.

10. "A nos lecteurs," *Annales d'histoire économique et sociale* 1 (1929), 1–2.

11. Febvre to the Collège de France and Bloch to the Sorbonne as successor to Henri Hauser as professor of social and economic history.

12. Published posthumously as *La Société Féodale*, 2 vols. (Paris, 1939–40), in 1946; the English translation was published in London in 1949.

13. Marc Bloch, *Feudal Society* (London, 1961).

14. Lucien Lefebvre, *The Problem of Unbelief in the Sixteenth Century: The Religion of Rabelais* (Cambridge, Mass., 1983).

15. Fernand Braudel, *The Mediterranean and The Mediterranean World in the Age of Philip II*, 2 vols. (New York, 1972–74).

16. Emmanuel Le Roy Ladurie, *Peasants of Languedoc* (Urbana, 1974).

17. Emmanuel Le Roy Ladurie, *Montaillou* (New York, 1978).

18. Fernand Braudel, *Civilisation matérielle, économie, capitalisme*, 3 vols. (Paris, 1979–87), English: *Civilization and Capitalism*, 3 vols. (New York, 1992).

19. Fernand Braudel, *The Identity of France*, 2 vols. (New York, 1988-90).

20. See Reinhard Koselleck, *Futures Past: On the Semantics of Historical Time* (Cambridge, Mass., 1985).

21. Reprinted in Jacques Le Goff, *Time, Work, and Culture in the Middle Ages* (Chicago, 1980).

22. E.g., Pierre Goubert, *Beauvais et le Beauvaisis de 1660 à 1730* (Paris 1960); René Baehrel, *Une Croissance: La Basse-Provence rurale fin XVIe siècle–1789* (Paris, 1961); Emmanuel Le Roy Ladurie, *Peasants of Languedoc*.

23. Fernand Braudel, *Structures of Everyday Life* (London, 1981); a version of the first volume of *Civilization and Capitalism*.

24. Marc Bloch, *French Rural History* (Berkeley, 1966).

25. "The Advent and the Triumph of the Watermill," in Marc Bloch, *Land and Work in Medieval Europe: Selected Papers* (Berkeley, 1967), 136–68.

26. Ernest Labrousse, *Histoire économique et sociale de la France*, 4 vols. (Paris, 1970–80).
27. See Emmanuel Le Roy Ladurie, *The Territory of the Historian* (Chicago, 1979); also François Furet, "Quantitative History," in Felix Gilbert, *Historical Studies Today* (New York, 1972); Pierre Chaunu, *Histoire quantitive, histoire sérielle* (Paris, 1978).
28. Ladurie, *The Territory of the Historian*, 285.
29. Emmanuel Le Roy Ladurie, *Histoire du climat* (Paris, 1967), English: *Times of Feast, Times of Famine* (New York, 1971).
30. Philippe Ariès, *Centuries of Childhood* (New York, 1965).
31. Philippe Ariès, *The Hour of Our Death* (London, 1981).
32. Robert Mandrou, *Magistrats et sorciers en France du XVIIe siècle* (Paris, 1968); *Les Fuggers, propriétaire fonciers en Souabes 1500–1618: Etude de comportements socio-économique a la fin du XVI siècle* (Paris, 1968).
33. Jacques Le Goff, *Time, Work, and Culture in the Middle Ages* (Chicago, 1980); *The Birth of Purgatory* (London, 1984).
34. E.g., Georges Duby, *The Knight, the Lady, and the Priest: The Making of Modern Marriage in Medieval France* (Chicago, 1993); *The Three Orders of Feudal Society Imagined* (Chicago, 1982); on the battle of Bouvines and its role in French historical memory, see *The Legend of Bouvines* (Cambridge, 1990).
35. See Pierre Chaunu et al., *La Mort à Paris* (Paris, 1978); also his *Histoire quantitative, histoire sérielle*.
36. Michel Vovelle, *Piété baroque et déchristianisation* (Paris, 1973); see also *Ideologies and Mentalities* (Cambridge, 1990),
37. See Lutz Raphael,"The Present as a Challenge to the Historian: The Contemporary World in the *Annales d'histoire economique et sociale*," *Storia della Storiografia* 21 (1992), 25–44.
38. Adeline Daumard, *La Bourgeoisie parisienne de 1815–1848* (Paris, 1963).
39. Jean Bouvier, *Crédit Lyonnais de 1863 à 1882* (Paris, 1963).
40. Charles Morazé, *Les Bourgeois conquérants* (Paris, 1957), English: *The Triumph of the Middle Classes* (Garden City, 1968).
41. Louis Chevalier, *Classes labourieuses et classes dangereuse à Paris pendant la première moitié du XIXe siècle* (Paris, 1958).
42. Maurice Agulhon, *La République au village* (Paris, 1970). On political symbolism, also see his *Marianne au Combat* (Paris, 1979), English: *Marianne into Battle: Republican Imagery and Symbolism in France 1789–1880* (Cambridge, 1981).
43. Mona Ozouf, *La Fête révolutionnaire, 1789–1799* (Paris, 1976), English: *Festivals and the French Revolution* (Cambridge, Mass., 1988).

44. Marc Ferro, *La Grande guerre* (Paris, 1969).
45. Marc Ferro, *La Révolution russe* (Paris, 1967).
46. E.g., François Furet, *Interpreting the French Revolution* (Cambridge, 1981).
47. Pierre Nora, ed., *Les Lieux des mémoires*, 3 vols. (Paris).
48. Aaron Gurevich, *Categories of Medieval Culture* (London, 1985).
49. See Georg G. Iggers, *New Directions in European Historiography*, 2d ed. (Middletown, Conn., 1984, 138–42.

6. Critical Theory and Social History: "Historical Social Science" in the Federal Republic of Germany (pp. 65–77)

1. See below, p. 97.
2. See Berndt Faulenbach, *Ideologie des deutschen Weges: Die deutsche Geschichte in der Historiographie zwischen Kaiserreich und Nationalsozialismus* (München, 1980).
3. Fritz Fischer, *Germany's War Aims in the First War* (New York, 1967).
4. For a history of the institute see Helmut Heiber, *Walter Frank und sein Reichsinstitut für Geschichte des Neuen Deutschlands* (Stuttgart, 1966).
5. Eckart Kehr, *Der Primat der Innenpolitik*, ed. Hans-Ulrich Wehler (Berlin, 1965).
6. Eckart Kehr, *Schlachtflottenbau und Parteipolitik 1894–1901* (Berlin, 1930, 1966).
7. See Wehler's "Einleitung" to vol. 1, *Deutsche Gesellschaftsgeschichte* (München, 1987–), 6–31. Three of the four projected volumes have now appeared.
8. Hans Ulrich Wehler, *Das Deutsche Kaiserreich* (Göttingen, 1973), 17, English: *The German Empire, 1871–1918* (Leamington Spa, 1985).
9. See Geoff Eley and David Blackbourn, *The Peculiarities of German History: Bourgeois Culture in 19th-Century Germany* (Oxford, 1984); also Thomas Nipperdey, *Deutsche Geschichte 1800–1866* (München, 1983) and *Deutsche Geschichte 1866–1918*, 2 vols. (München, 1993) .
10. See Hans Ulrich Wehler, *Historische Sozialwissenschaft und Geschichtsschreibung* (Göttingen, 1980).
11. See Georg G. Iggers, *The German Conception of History: The National Tradition of Historical Thought from Herder to the Present*, 2d ed. (Middletown, Conn., 1983).

12. See Georg G. Iggers, *The Social History of Politics: Critical Perspectives in West German Historical Writing Since 1945* (Leamington Spa, 1985), particularly Introduction, 1–48.

13. Subtitle of the journal is *Zeitschrift für Historische Sozialwissenschaft* (*Journal for Historical Social Science*).

14. Thomas Nipperdey, *Deutsche Geschichte 1800–1866* (München, 1983) and *Deutsche Geschichte 1866–1918*, 2 vols. (München, 1990–92).

15. *Unternehmensverwaltung und Angestelltenschaft am Beispiel Siemens 1847–1914: Zum Verhältnis von Kapitalismus und Bürokratie in der deutschen Industrialisierung* (Stuttgart, 1969).

16. Jürgen Kocka, *White Collar Workers in America: A Social-Political History in International Perspective* (London, 1980).

17. Very recently *Weder Stand noch Klasse: Unterschichten um 1800* (Bonn, 1990), first of a multivolume *Geschichre der Arbeiter und der Arbeiterbewegung seit dem Ende des 18. Jahrhunderts.*

18. Dieter Langewiesche and Klaus Schoenhorn, eds., *Arbeiter in Deutschland: Studien zur Lebensweise der Arbeiterschaft im Zeitalter der Industrialisierung* (Paderborn, 1981).

19. Franz-Josef Brüggemeier, *Leben vor Ort. Ruhrbergleute und Ruhrbergbau 1889–1919* (München, 1983). On environmental aspects, see his *Blauer Himmel über der Ruhr: Geschichte der Umwelt im Ruhrgebier, 1840–1990* (Essen, 1992).

20. See, e.g., Klaus Tenfelde and Gerald D. Feldmann eds., *Workers, Owners, and Politics in Coal Mining: An International Comparison of Industrial Relations* (New York, 1990).

21. Michelle Perrot, *Workers on Strike: France, 1871–1890* (New York, 1987).

22. See below, p. 129.

23. Lutz Niethammer, *Lebensgeschichte und Sozialkultur im Ruhrgebiet 1930 bis 1960*, 2 vols. (Berlin, 1983); a parallel investigation was carried out by Niethammer, Alexander von Plato, and Dorothee Wierling, *Die volkseigene Erfahrung: Eine Archäologie des Lebens in der Industrieprovinz DDR. 30 biographische Eröffnungen* (Berlin, 1990).

24. *Geschichte der deutschen Arbeiterbewegung in acht Bänden*, published by the Institute for Marxism-Leninism at Central Committee of the Socialist Unity Party, 8 vols. (Berlin, 1966).

25. Jürgen Kuczynski, *Geschichte des Alltags des Deutschen Volkes 1600–1945* (Berlin, 1981–82). For a discussion of social history in the GDR in the 1980s, see Georg G. Iggers, ed., *Marxist Historiography in Transformation: East German Social History in the 1980s*

(New York, 1991), particularly the introduction. The volume includes selections from East German writings from the 1980s, including an excerpt from Kuczynski's introduction to his *Alltagsgeschichte*.

26. Hartmut Zwahr, *Zur Konstituierung des Proletariats als Klasse: Strukturuntersuchungen über das Leipziger Proletariat während der industriellen Revolution* (Berlin, 1978).
27. See Georg G. Iggers, *Marxist Historiography in Transformation*.
28. See Joan W. Scott, "Women's History," in Peter Burke, *New Perspectives on Historical Writing* (State College, Penna., 1991), 42–66.
29. Dorothee Wierling, *Mädchen für alles: Arbeitstag und Lebensgeschichte städtischer Dienstmädchern um die Jahrhundertwende* (Berlin, 1987).

7. Marxist Historical Science from Historical Materialism to Critical Anthropology (pp. 78–94)

1. In Robert C. Tucker, ed., *The Marx-Engels Reader*, 2d ed. (New York. 1978), 3–6.
2. In Tucker, 66–125.
3. Karl Marx, *Capital, A Critique of Political Economy* (New York, 1967) vol. 1, 81.
4. From "Preface" *To a Critique of Political Economy* in Tucker, 5.
5. See Georg G. Iggers, *Marxist Historiography in Transformation: East German Social History in the 1980s* (New York, 1991), especially "Introduction," 1–37; also Andreas Dorpalen's very balanced and comprehensive examination of historical studies in the GDR, *German History in Marxist Perspective: The East German Approach* (Detroit, 1985).
6. See Georg G. Iggers, *New Directions in European Historiography*, 2d ed. (Middletown, 1984), 138–42.
7. Witold Kula, *Economic Theory of the Feudal System* (London, 1976).
8. Witold Kula, *Miary i Ludzie* (Warsaw, 1970).
9. See Mikhail M. Bakhtin, *Rabelais and His World* (Cambridge, Mass., 1968).
10. Aaron Gurevich, *The Categories of Medieval Culture* (Boston, 1985).
11. See Iggers, *Marxist Historiography in Transformation*.
12. Institut für Marxismus-Leninismus beim Zentralkomitee der SED, *Geschichte der deutschen Arbeiterbewegung* (Berlin, 1966), vol. 1, 7.

Notes • 175

13. Jürgen Kuczynski, *Geshichte des Alltags des deutschen Volkes, 1600–1945*, 5 vols. (Berlin 1981-82). See translation of excerpts of Kuczynski's "Preface" in Iggers, *Marxist Historiography in Transformation*, 38–42.
14. See Harvey J. Kaye, *The British Marxist Historians* (Cambridge, 1984). Also Eric Hobsbawm, "The Historians' Group of the Communist Party," in M. Cornforth, ed., *Rebels and their Causes* (London, 1978), 21-48.
15. See Kaye, *The British Marxist Historians*, 42–50. An important part of this debate was carried out in the American Marxist journal *Science and Society*.
16. See Kaye, *The British Marxist Historians*, 16.
17. "The Eighteenth Brumaire of Louis Bonaparte," in Robert C. Tucker, ed., *The Marx-Engels Reader*, 1st ed. (New York, 1972), 515.
18. See ibid., 479.
19. Georges Lefebvre, *The Great Fear of 1789: Rural Panic in Revolutionary France* (New York, 1972).
20. On Hilton, see Kaye, *The British Marxist Historians*. Also Hilton, *The Transition from Feudalism to Capitalism* (London, 1976).
21. E.g., Christopher Hill, *The World Turned Upside Down: Radical Ideas During the English Revolution* (Harmondsworth, 1975).
22. W. E. B. Du Bois, *Black Reconstruction in America: An Essay on the Role which Black Folks Played in the Attempt to Reconstruct Democracy in America 1860–1920* (New York, 1935).
23. George Rudé, *The Crowd in the French Revolution* (New York, 1959).
24. Among an extensive list of Richard Cobb's writings, see *The Police and the People: French Popular Protest, 1789–1820* (New York, 1975); *Death in Paris: The Records of the Baisse-Geole de la Seine, October 1795 to September 1801* (Oxford, 1978).
25. George Rudé, "The Moral Economy of the English Crowd in the Eighteenth-Century," *Past and Present*, 50 (1971), 76–136.
26. Eric Hobsbawm, *Primitive Rebels: Studies in Archaic Forms of Social Movement in the Nineteenth and Twentieth Centuries* (New York, 1963).
27. George Rudé, *Captain Swing* (New York, 1968).
28. Eric Hobsbawm, *The Age of Revolution, 1789–1848* (Cleveland, 1962); *The Age of Capital* (London, 1975); *The Age of Empire, 1875-1914* (New York, 1987); *The Age of Extremes: A History of the World, 1914–1991* (New York, 1994).
29. E. P. Thompson, *The Making of the English Working Class* (New York, 1966), Preface, 9.

30. See Thompson, *The Poverty of Theory and Other Essays* (London, 1978).
31. Ibid., pp. 380, 383.
32. *Making of the English Working Class*, Preface, 9.
33. Ibid.
34. Ibid., 10.
35. Ibid., 12–13.
36. See also Thompson's reconstruction of plebean culture in the essays collected in *Customs in Common* (London, 1991).
37. Joan Wallach Scott, "Women in *The Making of the English Working Class*," in Scott, *Gender and the Politics of History* (New York, 1988), 68–90.
38. Louis Althusser, *For Marx* (New York, 1969), 97.
39. Gareth Stedman Jones, *Language of Class* (Cambridge, 1983), 101–102.
40. "The Attack," *History Workshop* 4 (Autumn 1977), 1–4.
41. Ibid., 4.
42. "History Workshop Journal," *History Workshop* 1 (Spring 1976), 1.
43. Ibid, 4–6.
44. Ibid., 9–25.
45. "Workshop of the World: Steam Power and Hand Technology in Mid-Victorian Britain," *History Workshop* (Spring 1977), 6–72.
46. *History Workshop* 20 (Autumn 1985), 1–4.
47. "Language and History," *History Workshop* 10 (Autumn 1980), 1–5.
48. Ibid., 175–83.
49. "Work and Its Representations: A Research Proposal," ibid., 164–74.
50. "Ten Years After," *History Workshop* 20 (Autumn 1985), 1–4.
51. "Change and Continuity," *History Workshop* (Spring 1995), iii–iv.

8. Lawrence Stone and "The Revival of Narrative"
(pp. 97–100)

1. Lawrence Stone, "The Revival of Narrative: Reflections on a New Old History," *Past and Present* 85 (November 1979), 3–24.
2. Ibid., 19.
3. Ibid., 9.
4. John Kenneth Galbraith, *The Affluent Society* (Boston, 1960).
5. Daniel Bell, *The End of Ideology: On the Exhaustion of Political Ideas in the Fifties* (Glencoe, Ill. 1960).

6. Michael Harrington, *The Other America: Poverty in the United States* (New York, 1962).
7. The French title *Le dimanche de Bouvines: 27 juillet 1214* (The Sunday at Bouvines) stressed both the events of one day, July 27, 1214, and their projection into historical consciousness.
8. Jacques Le Goff, *St. Louis* (Paris, 1996).
9. See Art Berman, *From the New Criticism to Deconstruction* (Urbana, 1988).

9. From Macro- to Microhistory: The History of Everyday Life (pp. 101–17)

1. Francis Fukuyama, "The End of History?," *The National Interest*, vol. 9 (Summer 1989), 3–18.
2. Jürgen Kocka, *Vereinigungskrise: Zur Geschichte der Gegenwart* (Göttingen, 1995).
3. See Edward Muir and Guido Ruggiero, eds., *Microhistory and the Lost Peoples of Europe* (Baltimore, 1991).
4. Fernand Braudel, *The Structures of Everyday Life* (London, 1981), the first volume of his three-volume *Material Civilization and Capitalism*.
5. Wilhelm Riehl, *Die Naturgeschichte des Volkes als Grundlage einer deutschen Social-Politik* (Stuttgart, 1856).
6. E. P. Thompson, *The Making of the English Working Class* (New York, 1966), 12.
7. E.g., George Duby, *The Knight, the Lady, and the Priest: The Making of Modern Marriage in Medieval France* (Chicago, 1993); *The Three Orders: Feudal Society Imagined* (Chicago, 1980).
8. E.g., Jacques Le Goff, *Intellectuals in the Middle Ages* (Cambridge, Mass., 1993).
9. George Duby, *The Legend of Bouvines* (Cambridge, Mass., 1990).
10. Jacques Le Goff, *St. Louis* (Paris, 1996).
11. Keith Thomas, *Religion and the Decline of Magic: Studies in Popular Beliefs in 16th and 17th Century Europe* (London, 1971).
12. Peter Burke, *Popular Culture in Early Modern Europe* (London, 1978).
13. Natalie Z. Davis, *Society and Culture in Early Modern France* (New York, 1975).
14. Carlo Ginzburg, *The Cheese and the Worms: The Cosmos of a Sixteenth-Century Miller* (New York, 1978).

15. See Jürgen Kocka, *Sozialgeschichte, Begriff, Entwicklung, Probleme*, 2d ed. (Göttingen, 1986), 162–174.
16. Hans Medick, "Missionaries in the Row Boat," *Comparative Studies in Society and History* 29 (1987), 76–98.
17. Clifford Geertz, "Thick Description: Toward an Interpretive Theory of Culture," ch. 1 in Geertz, *The Interpretations of Cultures* (New York, 1973), 3–30.
18. Hans Medick, "Entlegene Geschichte? Sozialgeschichte im Blickfeld der Kulturanthropologie," in Konrad Jarausch et al., eds., *Geschichtswissenschaft vor 2000: Persspektiven der Historiographiegeschichte. Festschrift für Georg G. Iggers zum 65. Geburtstag* (Hagen, 1991), 360–69.
19. Franklin Mendels, "Proto-Industrialization: The First Phase of the Industrialization Process," *Journal of Economic History* 32 (1972), 241–61.
20. For a discussion of the literature, see Richard L. Rudolph, ed., *The European Peasant Family and Society: Historical Studies* (Liverpool, 1995).
21. Peter Kriedte, Hans Medick, Jürgen Schlumbohm, eds., *Industrialization Before Industrialization* (Cambridge, 1981).
22. Hans Medick, "Plebeian Culture in the Transition to Capitalism," in Ralph Samuel and Gareth Stedman Jones, eds., *Culture, Ideology, and Politics: Essays for Eric Hobsbawm*, History Workshop Series (London, 1982), 84–112.
23. Hans Medick, *Weben und Überleben in Laichingen 1650–1900: Lokalgeschichte als Allgemeine Geschichte (Göttingen, 1996).*
24. David Sabean, *Property, Production and Family in Neckarhausen 1700–1870*, vol. 1 (Cambridge, 1990).
25. Jürgen Schlumbohm, *Lebensläufe. Familien. Höfe. Die Bauern und Eigentumslosen des Osnabrückischen Kirchspiels Belm in proto-industrieller Zeit 1650–1860* (Göttingen, 1994).
26. On the Italian microhistorians, see Giovanni Levi, "On Microhistory," in Peter Burke, ed., *New Perspectives on Historical Writing* (University Park, Penna., 1991), 93–113; and Edward Muir and Guido Ruggiero, *Microhistory and the Lost People of Europe: Selections from* Quaderni Storici (Baltimore, 1991).
27. Giovanni Levi, *Inheriting Power: The Story of an Exorcist* (Chicago, 1988).
28. Natalie Davis, *Fiction in the Archives: Pardon Tales and their Tellers in Sixteenth-Century France* (Stanford, 1987).
29. "Mikro-Historie: Zwei oder drei Dinge, die ich von ihr weiß,"

Historische Anthropologie. Kultur, Gesellschaft. Alltag 1 (1993), 169–92.

30. Edward Muir, "Introduction: Observing Trifles," in Muir and Ruggiero, eds., *Microhistory and the Lost Peoples of Europe,* xxi.
31. Ibid., 13.
32. Ginzburg, *The Cheese and the Worms.*
33. Giovanni Levi, *Inheriting Power: The Story of an Exorcist* (Chicago, 1988).
34. Muir, "Introduction," xvi.
35. Levi, "On Microhistory," 106.
36. Ibid.
37. Ibid.
38. Muir, "Introduction," xiii.
39. Ibid.
40. Ibid., 103.
41. Ibid., 105.
42. Levi, *Inheriting Power,* back cover of paperback edition.
43. David Sabean, *Property, Production, and Family in Neckarhausen 1700–1870,* vol. 1 (Cambridge, 1990).
44. Eric Wolf, *Europe and the Peoples Without a History* (Berkeley, 1982).
45. Sydney Mintz, *Sweetness and Power: Sugar in Modern History* (New York, 1985).
46. Norbert Elias, *The Civilizing Process* (New York, 1978).
47. See Alf Lüdtke, ed., *The History of Everyday Life: Reconstructing Historical Experiences and Ways of Life* (Princeton, 1995).
48. Alf Lüdtke, "'Coming to Terms with the Past': Illusions of Remembering Ways of Forgetting Nazism in West Germany," *Journal of Modern History* 65 (1993), 542–72.
49. Lutz Niethammer, ed., *Lebensgeschichte und Sozialkultur im Ruhrgebiet 1930 bis 1960,* 2 vols. (Berlin, 1983).
50. Lutz Niethammer, Alexander von Plato, and Dorothee Wierling, eds., *Die volkseigene Erfahrung: Eine Archäologie des Lebens in der Industrieprovinz der DDR* (Berlin, 1990).
51. Christopher R. Browning, "German Memory, Judicial Interrogation, and Historical Reconstruction: Writing Perpetrator History From Postwar Testimony," in Saul Friedlander, ed., *Probing the Limits of Representation: Nazism and the "Final Solution"* (Cambridge, Mass., 1992), 35.
52. Christopher R. Browning, *Ordinary Men: Reserve Police Battalion 101 and the Final Solution in Poland* (New York, 1992).

53. Raoul Hilberg, *The Destruction of the European Jews* (Chicago, 1961).
54. Hannah Arendt *Eichmann in Jerusalem: A Report on the Banality of Evil* (New York, 1963).
55. Browning, "German Memory," in Friedlander, ed., *Probing the Limits of Representation*, 350.
56. Hayden White, "Historical Emplotment and the Problem of Truth," in Friedlander, ed., *Probing the Limits of Representation*, 37–53.
57. Browning, "German Memory," ibid., 31.

10. The "Linguistic Turn": The End of History as a Scholarly Discipline? (pp. 118–34)

1. Lawrence Stone, "The Revival of Narrative," *Past and Present* 85 (November 1979): 19.
2. Roland Barthes, "The Discourse of History," *Comparative Criticism: A Yearbook*, vol. 3 (1981), 3–28.
3. Hayden White, "Historical Texts as Literary Artifact," in *Tropes of Discourse* (Baltimore, 1978), 82.
4. Natalie Davis, *The Return of Martin Guerre* (Cambridge, Mass., 1983).
5. Patrick Bahners, "Die Ordnung der Geschichte: Über Hayden White," *Merkur* 46, (1992) Heft 6 (1992), 313.
6. Gaston Bachelard, *The New Scientific Spirit* (Boston, 1984).
7. Paul Feyeraband, *Against Method* (London, 1988).
8. Thomas Kuhn, *The Structure of Scientific Revolutions*, 2d ed. (Chicago, 1970).
9. Ferdinand de Saussure, *Course in General Linguistics* (London, 1983).
10. See Art Berman, *From the New Criticism to Deconstruction* (Urbana, 1988).
11. Barthes, "Discourse of History."
12. Dominick La Capra, "Rhetoric and History," in *History and Criticism* (Ithaca, 1985), 15–44.
13. Ibid., 42.
14. See "On the Character of Historical Science," in Leopold von Ranke, *Theory and Practice of History*, 33–34.
15. See J. E. Toews, "Intellectual History After the Linguistic Turn: The Autonomy of Meaning and the Irreducibility of Experience," *American Historical Review* 92 (1987), 879–907; Martin Jay,

"Should Intellectual History Take a Linguistic Turn? Reflections on the Habermas-Gadamer Debate," in Dominick La Capra and Steven Kaplan, eds., *Modern European Intellectual History. Reappraisals and New Perspectives* (Ithaca, 1982), 86–110; Richard Rorty, ed., *The Linguistic Turn: Recent Essays in Philosophic Method* (Chicago, 1967).

16. Clifford Geertz, "Thick Description: Toward an Interpretive Theory of Culture" in his *The Interpretation of Cultures* (New York, 1983), 5.

17. See "'Objectivity' in Social Science and Social Policy," in Edward A. Shils and Henry A. Finch, eds., *Max Weber on the Methodology of the Social Sciences* (Glencoe, Ill., 1949).

18. Geertz, "Thick Description," 5.

19. Clifford Geertz, "Deep Play: Notes on the Balinese Cockfight," in *Interpretation of Cultures*, 412–53.

20. "Captain James Cook; or the Dying God," in Sahlins, *Islands of History* (Chicago, 1987), 104–35.

21. Robert Darnton, *The Great Cat Massacre and Other Episodes in French Cultural History* (New York, 1984).

22. Roger Chartier, "Texts, Symbols, and Frenchness," *Journal of Modern History* 57 (1985), 684.

23. Emmanuel Le Roy Ladurie, *Carnival in Romans* (New York, 1979).

24. Geertz, "Thick Description," 5; see also his definition of culture, "Religion as a Cultural System," ibid., 89.

25. J. G. A. Pocock, *The Machiavellian Moment: Florentine Political Thought and the Atlantic Republican Tradition* (Princeton, 1975), and *Politics, Language, and Time: Essays on Political Thought and History* (Chicago, 1989).

26. Quentin Skinner, *The Foundations of Modern Political Thought: The Renaissance*, 2 vols. (Cambridge, 1989).

27. Jürgen Habermas, *The Theory of Communicative Action* (Boston, 1984).

28. Reinhard Koselleck, *Futures Past: On the Semantics of Historical Time* (Cambridge Mass., 1985).

29. *Geschichtliche Grundbegriffe* (Stuttgart, 1972–). The encyclopedia is complete except for an eighth index volume.

30. Régine Robin, *La Société française en 1789: Semur-en-Anxois* (Paris, 1970), and *Histoire et linguistique* (Paris, 1973).

31. Lynn Hunt, *Politics, Culture, and Class in the French Revolution* (Berkeley, 1984), xi.

32. François Furet, "Le Catéchisme révolutionnaire," *Annales. Economies. Sociétés. Civilisations.* 26 (1971), 255–89.

33. Alfred Cobban, *The Social Interpretation of the French Revolution* (Cambridge, 1965).

34. George Taylor, "The Paris Bourse on the Eve of the Revolution 1781–1789," *American Historical Review* 67 (1961–62), 951–77.

35. Albert Soboul, *The French Revolution 1787–1799* (New York, 1974), and *The Parisian Sans Culottes* (Oxford, 1964).

36. Georges Lefebvre, *The French Revolution*, 2 vols. (London, 1962–64), and *The Coming of the French Revolution* (Princeton, 1947).

37. See F. Furet and Mona Ozouf, eds., *The Transformation of Political Culture 1789–1843*, 3 vols. (Oxford, 1989).

38. Maurice Agulhon, *La République au village* (Paris, 1970), and *Marianne into Battle: Republican Imagery in France 1789–1880* (Cambridge, 1981).

39. Mona Ozouf, *La Fête révolutionnaire 1789–1799* (Paris, 1976).

40. William Sewell, *Work and Revolution in France: The Language of Labor from the Old Regime to 1848* (Cambridge, 1980).

41. Ibid., 10–11.

42. Gareth Stedman Jones, *Languages of Class: Studies in English Working Class History 1832–1982* (Cambridge, 1983), 101. See also B. Stråth, ed., *Language and the Construction of Class Identities* (Gothenburg, 1990).

43. Thomas Childers, "The Social Language of Politics in Germany: The Sociology of Political Discourse in the Weimar Republic," *American Historical Review* 95 (1990), 331–58.

44. Ibid., 337.

45. See Joan Scott's "Introduction" to *Gender and the Politics of History* (New York, 1988), 1–11.

46. Joan Scott, "On Language, Gender, and Working Class History," ibid., 53–67.

47. William Sewell, review essay of Joan Wallack Scott, *Gender and the Politics of History*, *History and Theory* 29 (1990), 79.

48. Letter from Joan W. Scott to Georg G. Iggers, October 14, 1994.

49. E.g., Joan Scott, "French Feminists and the Rights of 'Man': Olympes de Gouges' Declarations," *History Workshop* 28 (Autumn 1989), 1–22.

50. Lynn Hunt, ed., *New Cultural History* (Berkeley, 1989).

51. Stedman Jones, *Languages of Class*, 95.

52. Quoted in Berman, *From the New Criticism*, 183.

53. Carroll Smith-Rosenberg, "The Body Politic," in E. Weed, ed., *Feminism/Theory/Politics* (New York, 1989), 101.

Notes · **183**

11. From the Perspective of the 1990s (pp. 134–40)

1. Lawrence Stone, "History and Post-Modernism," *Past and Present* 131 (August 1991), 217–18.
2. Ibid., 217.
3. Patrick Joyce, "History and Post-Modernism," *Past and Present* 133 (November 1991), 208.
4. Lawrence Stone, "History and Post-Modernism III," *Past and Present* 135 (May 1992), 191.
5. Simon Schama, *Dead Certainties: Unwarranted Speculations* (New York, 1991).
6. Jonathan Spence, *The Question of Hu* (New York, 1988).
7. "Histoire, Sciences Sociales," *Annales* 49 (1994), 3–4. I am thankful to Marc Ferro, a longtime editor of the *Annales*, for a long interview in April 1995 on the discussions leading to the change of title.
8. See "Histoire et sciences sociales. Un tournant critique?," *Annales* 43 (1988), 291–93.
9. Jacques Revel, "Histoire et sciences sociales: Une confrontation instable," in Jean Boutier and Dominique Julia, eds., *Passés recomposés: Champs et chantiers de l'Histoire* (Paris, 1995), 80.
10. See Edoardo Grendi's notion of "the exceptional normal" cited in Giovanni Levi, "On Microhistory," in Peter Burke, ed., *New Perspectives in Historical Writing* (State University, Penna., 1991) 109, and Edward Muir and Guido Ruggiero, *Microhistory and the Lost People of Europe* (Baltimore, 1991), "Introduction," xiv.
11. "Le Temps des doutes," *Le Monde*, March 18, 1993, vi–vii.
12. E.g., Alfred Heuss, *Der Verlust der Geschichte* (Göttingen, 1959).
13. Indicative of current debates are the publications of the National Center for History in the Schools (Los Angeles, 1995): *National Standards for United States History for Grades K–4*; *National Standards for United States History for Grades 5–12*; and *National Standards for World History.*

Concluding Remarks (pp. 141–47)

1. See Lutz Niethammer, *Posthistoire: Has History Ended?* (London, 1992).
2. Francis Fukuyama, *The End of History and the Last Man* (New York, 1992).
3. Søren Kierkegaard, *The Present Age* (New York, 1962).

4. J. G. Droysen, *Outline of the Principles of History* (Boston, 1893).
5. Oswald Spengler, *The Decline of the West,* 2 vols. (New York, 1926–28).
6. Arnold Toynbee, *A Study of History* 10 vols. (New York, 1947–57).
7. See Eric Wolf, *Europe and the People Without History* (Berkeley, 1982).
8. See Peter Novick, *That Noble Dream* (Cambridge, 1988).
9. Natalie Davis, *The Return of Martin Guerre* (Cambridge, Mass., 1983).
10. See Hans Kellner's yet unpublished presentation at the 18th International Congress of Historical Sciences, Montreal, 1995; also his *Language and Historical Representation: Getting the Story Crooked* (Madison, 1989).
11. F. A. Ankersmit, "Historicism: An Attempt at Synthesis," *History and Theory* 34 (1995), 155.
12. Novick, *That Noble Dream.*
13. Max Horkheimer and Theodor W. Adorno, *The Dialectic of Enlightenment* (New York, 1972).
14. Jean-Antoine-Nicolas de Caritat, marquis de Condorcet, *Sketch for a Historical Picture of the Progress of the Human Mind* (New York, 1955).
15. Cf. Gerhard Ritter, *The German Problem: Basic Questions of German Political Life, Past and Present* (Columbus, Ohio, 1965); J. L. Talmon, *The Origins of Totalitarian Democracy* (New York, 1960); also Hannah Arendt, *The Origins of Totalitarianism* (New York, 1951), and Friedrich Hayek, *Road to Serfdom* (Chicago, 1994).

Epilogue: A Retrospect at the Beginning of the Twenty-First Century (pp. 149–60)

1. For a succinct assessment of recent trends, see *Journal of Social History* 37 (2003), particularly Peter N. Stearns, "Social History Present and Future," 9–20; Jürgen Kocka, "Losses, Gains and Opportunities," 21–28; Hartmut Kaelble, "Social History in Europe: Introducing the Issues," 29–37; Paula S. Fass, "Cultural History/Social History," 39–46; Prasannan Parthasarathi, "The State of Indian Social History," 47–56; Christophe Charle, "Contemporary French Social History," 57–68. On labor history see Marcel van der Linden, 69–76, as well as other articles. Also see Stefan Berger, Heiko Feldner, and Kevin Passmore, eds., *Writing History: Theory and Practice* (London, 2003).
2. Ernst Breisach, *On the Future of History: The Postmodernist Chal-*

lenge and Its Aftermath (Chicago, 2003). See also Richard J. Evans, *In Defence of History*, new edition with a response to his critics (London, 2001).

3. Keith Jenkins, ed., *The Postmodern History Reader* (London, 1997), 6. See also Perez Zagorin's reaction to Jenkins's volume, "History, the Referent, and Narrative: Reflections on Postmodernism Now," *History and Theory* 38 (1999): 1–24; and Jenkins, "A Postmodern Reply to Perez Zagorin," *History and Theory* 39 (2000): 181–200.

4. Robert Anchor, "The Quarrel Between Historians and Postmodernists," *History and Theory* 38 (1999): 111–21, a review of Chris Lorenz, *Konstruktion der Vergangenheit: Eine Einführung in die Geschichtstheorie* (Cologne, 1997).

5. See J. D. Faubion, "Anthropology and History," in *International Encyclopedia of the Social and Behavioral Sciences* (henceforth to be cited as *IESBS*) (Amsterdam, 2001), 519–23; William M. Reddy, "Anthropology and the History of Culture," in Lloyd Kramar and Sarah Maza, eds., *A Companion to Western Historical Thought* (London, 2002), 277–96.

6. See Melvin Richter, *The History of Political and Social Concepts* (New York, 1995).

7. For a later formulation of Scott's position, see "After History?" in Joan W. Scott and Debra Keates, eds., *Schools of Thought: Twenty-Five Years of Interpretive Social Science* (Princeton, 2001), 85–103.

8. James Sheehan, "Political History (History of Politics)," in *IESBS*, 11667–73.

9. See Q. Edward Wang, *Inventing China Through History: The May Fourth Approach to Historiography* (Albany, 2001).

10. See O. Chatterjee, "Subaltern History," *IESBS*, 15237–41; Vinay Lal, "The Subaltern School and the Ascendancy of Indian History," in Q. Edward Wang and Georg G. Iggers, *Turning Points in Historiography: A Cross Cultural Perspective* (Rochester, 2002), 237–70; Prasenjit Duara, "Postcolonial History," in Lloyd Kramer and Sarah Maza, eds., *A Companion to Western Historical Thought* (Oxford, 2002), 417–31.

11. K. Canning, "Gender History," in *IESBS*, 6822–29; N. Hewitt, "Gender and Feminist Studies in History," *IESBS*, 5929–33.

12. K. Canning, "Gender History," 6006–11.

13. A. Assmann, "History and Memory," in *IESBS*, 6822–29.

14. Chris Browning, *Ordinary Men: Reserve Battalion 101 and the Final Solution in Poland* (New York, 1992).

15. Pierre Nora, ed., *Les Lieux de Mémoire* (Paris, 1984–92). For English edition, see *Realms of Memory: Rethinking the French Past* (New

York, 1996–98). For a parallel volume for Germany, see Etienne François and Hagen Schulze, *Deutsche Erinnerungsorte*, 3 vols. (Munich, 2001).

16. Monika Flacke, ed., *Mythen der Nationen, Ein europäisches Panorama* (Berlin, 1998); Monika Flacke, ed., *Mythen der Nationen: 1945–Arena der Erinnerungen* (Berlin, 2004), publications of the Deutsches Historischen Museums to accompany exhibits.

17. Francis Fukuyama, *The End of History and the Last Man* (New York, 1992), xiv–xv, xii, xx.

18. P. Nolte, "Modernization and Modernity in History," in *IESBS*, 9954–61.

19. Samuel Huntington, *The Clash of Civilizations and the Remaking of World Order* (New York, 1996), 21.

20. Ibid., 20–21.

21. Jürgen Kocka, "Multiple Modernities and Negotiated Universals," in Dominic Sachsenmaier, Jens Riedel, and Shmuel N. Eisenstadt, *Reflections on Multiple Modernities: European, Chinese and Other Interpretations* (Leyden, 2002), 120.

22. E.g., Ashis Nandy, "History's Forgotten Doubles," in *History and Theory* Theme Issue 34 (1995): 44–66. On Postcolonialist thought on history, see Prajensit Duara, "Postcolonial History," in Lloyd Kramer and Sarah Maza, *A Companion to Western Historical Thought* (London, 2002), 417–31.

23. E.g., Hans-Ulrich Wehler, *The German Empire 1871–1918* (Leamington Spa, 1985).

24. E.g., Jeffrey Herf, *Reactionary Modernism: Technology, Culture and Politics in Weimar and in the Third Reich* (Cambridge, 1987).

25. E.g., Arnd Bauerkämper, "Geschichtsschreibung als Projektion: Die Revision der 'Whig Interpretation of History' und die Kritik am Paradigma vom 'deutschen Sonderweg' seit den 1970er Jahren" in Stefan Berger, Peter Lambert, and Peter Schumann, eds., *Historikertage: Geschichte, Mythos und Gedächtnis im deutsch-britischen kulturellen Austausch 1750–2000* (Göttingen, 2003), 383–438. Older works that already challenged the classical notion of modernization: Arno Mayer, *Persistence of the Old Regime* (New York, 1981); Alexander Gerschenkron, *Economic Backwardness in Historical Perspective* (Cambridge, Mass., 1962); Barrington Moore, *Social Origins of Dictatorship and Democracy: Lord and Peasant in the Making of the Modern World* (Boston, 1969).

26. Dipesh Chakrabarty, *Provincializing Europe: Postcolonial Thought and Historical Difference* (Princeton, 2000).

27. See Sachsenmaier et al., *Reflections on Multiple Modernities*.

28. Bruce Mazlish and Ralph Buultjens, *Conceptualizing Global History* (Boulder, 1993); see also the various articles on different aspects globalization and global history in *IESBS*.
29. See Jürgen Kocka, "Comparison and Beyond," *History and Theory* 42 (2003): 39–44; Chris Lorenz, "Comparative Historiography: Problems and Perspectives," *History and Theory* 38 (1999): 25–39.
30. Nandy, "History's Forgotten Doubles," 44.
31. Sumit Sarkar, "Post-modernism and the Writing of History," *(New Delhi) Studies in History* 15, 2, n.s. (1999): 293–322.
32. Mirjana Gross, *Von der Antike zur Postmoderne: Die zeitgenössische Geschichtsschreibung und ihre Wurzeln* (Wien, 1998); Michael Bentley, *Modern Historiography* (London, 1999); Anna Green and Kathleen Troup, eds., *The Houses of History: A Critical Reader in Twentieth-Century History and Theory* (New York, 1999); Hans-Ulrich Wehler, *Historisches Denken am Ende des 20: Jahrhunderts* (München, 2001); Lloyd Kramer and Sarah Maza, *A Companion to Western Historical Thought* (Oxford, 2002); Joachim Eibach and Günther Lottes, eds., *Kompass der Geschichtswissenschaft* (Göttingen, 2002); Donald Kelley, *Fortunes of History* (New Haven, 2003); Lutz Raphael, *Geschichtswissenschaft im Zeitalter der Extreme. Theorien, Methoden, Tendenzen von 1900 bis zur Gegenwart* (München, 2003). Briefly includes developments in the non-Western world. A truly global dictionary is Daniel Woolf, ed., *A Global Encyclopedia of Historical Writing*. 2 vols. (New York, 1998).
33. Jörn Rüsen and Achim Mittag, eds., *Die Vielfalt der Kulturen* (1998); Jörn Rüsen, ed., *Western Historical Thinking: An Intercultural Debate* (New York, 2002); Eckhardt Fuchs and Benedikt Stuchtey, eds., *Across Cultural Boundaries: Historiography in Global Perspective* (London, 2002); Q. Edward Wang and Georg G. Iggers, eds., *Turning Points in Historiography: A Cross Cultural Perspective* (Rochester, 2002); Benedikt Stuchtey and Eckhardt Fuchs, *Writing World History 1800–2000* (Oxford, 2003).
34. Two current historiographical projects that attempt an intercultural approach should be mentioned. Daniel Woolf, who recently edited the two volume *Global Dictionary of Historical Writing* (New York, 1998) has just completed a manuscript, "International Historiography," that will appear in the forthcoming new edition of *Dictionary of the History of Ideas.* Unlike the article on historiography by Herbert Butterfield in the previous edition of the *Dictionary of the History of Ideas* (New York, 1973), which except for a brief section on classical Chinese scholarship and a paragraph on Ibn Khaldoun focuses exclusively on the Western tradition, Woolf deals with historical writ-

ing in a large number of cultures since distant antiquity. With a large group of collaborators, Woolf now plans a comprehensive multi-volume global history of historiography. He carefully avoids Euro-centrism and seeks to present each culture on its own terms. Together with Q. Edward Wang I am now engaged in writing a comparative inter-global history of historiography since 1750, more limited in scope than Woolf's project, but concerned with the interaction of Western and non-Western historical thought in the age of European pene-tration of much of the non-Western world, which introduces a pro-nounced comparative perspective.

Suggested Readings

There does not exist a comprehensive overview of historical thought and historical writing in the twentieth century as there does for the nineteenth century in George P. Gooch, *History and Historians in the Nineteenth Century* (London, 1913). The present book is an attempt at partially filling the gap. I am aware of its limitations, both its selectivity and its failure to deal with historical studies outside Europe and North America. There are several important attempts to examine historical studies at a given point of time. Geoffrey Barraclough, in *History in a Changing World* (Oxford, 1955), dealt with what he considered to be a fundamental reorientation of historical thought and writing at the end of the colonial era. A number of books and special journal numbers in the 1970s and 1980s endeavored to take stock of the historiographical climate, including Felix Gilbert and Stephen R. Graubard, eds., *Historical Studies Today* (New York, 1972); Charles Delzell, ed., *The Future of History* (Nashville, 1977); Geoffrey Barraclough, *Main Trends in History* (New York, 1979); Theodore K. Rabb and Robert Rothberg, *The New History: The 1980's and Beyond* (Princeton, 1982); Georg G. Iggers, ed., "Social History at the End of the 1980's: A Critical International Perspective," *Storia della Storiografia*, issues 17 and 18 (1990); and Peter Burke, ed., *New Perspectives on Historical Writing* (State College, Penna., 1991). An examination of historical methodology as well as major trends in historical writing that extends beyond the Western world is contained in Georg G. Iggers and Harold T. Parker, *International Handbook of Historical Studies. Contemporary Research and Theory* (Westport, Conn., 1979). Fritz Stern, ed., *The Varieties of History from Voltaire to the Present* (New York, 1973), continues to be a good reader.

As for specific national developments in the late twentieth century, see Michael Kammen, *The Past Before Us: Contemporary Historical Writing in the United States* (Ithaca, 1980). On reorientations in French historical thought and practice, see Jacques Le Goff and Pierre Nora, *Constructing the Past: Essays in Historical Methodology* (Cambridge, Mass., 1984). The best although controversial examination of American traditions of historical writing from the beginnings of the American historical profession in the 1880s to the 1980s is in my opinion Peter Novick, *That Noble Dream: The "Objectivity Question" and the American Historical Profession* (Cambridge, Mass., 1988); for the first half of the twentieth century, Ernst Breisach, *American Progressive History: An Experiment in Modernization* (Chicago, 1993). For the social and intellectual setting of the social sciences in Germany in the first third of the twentieth century, see Fritz K. Ringer, *The Decline of the German Mandarins: The German Academic Community 1890–1933* (Cambridge, Mass., 1969; for post-1945 West Germany, Georg G. Iggers, ed., *The Social History of Politics: Critical Perspectives in West German Historical Writing Since 1945* (New York, 1986); on East Germany, Georg G. Iggers, *Marxist Historiography in Transformation: East German Social History in the 1980s* (New York, 1991). For France, on the *Annales*, Peter Burke, *The French Historical Revolution: The Annales School, 1929–89* (London, 1990); see also Bryce Lyon and Mary Lyon, *The Birth of Annales History: The Letters of Lucien Febvre and Marc Bloch to Henri Pirenne* (Brussels, 1991). For recent French assessments, see François Bédarida, *L'Histoire et le métier d'historien en France 1945–1995* (Paris, 1945–95), and Jean Boutier and Dominique Julia, *Passés recomposés: Champs et chantiers de l'histoire* (Paris, 1995).

There is an extensive literature on the challenge of postmodernism and linguistic theory to traditional forms of historiography. *History and Theory*, *The American Historical Review*, *The Journal of Modern History*, and *Past and Present* have been important forums for these discussions since the mid-1980s. A searching examination of the issues in these discussions is contained in Gabrielle M. Spiegel, "History, Historicism, and the Social Logic of the Text in the Middle Ages," *Speculum* 65 (1990), 59–86. See also John E. Toews, "Intellectual History After the Linguistic Turn: The Autonomy of Meaning and the Irreducibility of Experience," *American Historical Review* 92 (1987), 879–907. For very recent discussions of the current debates from very different positions see Joyce Appleby, Lynn Hunt, Margaret Jacob, *Telling the Truth about History* (New

York, 1994); Frank Ankersmit and Hans Kellner, *The New Philosophy of History* (Chicago, 1995); Robert F. Berkhofer, Jr., *Beyond the Great Story: History as Text and Discourse* (Cambridge, Mass., 1995); and very polemically, Gertrude Himmelfarb, *The New History and the Old* (Cambridge, Mass., 1987), and Keith Windshuttle, *The Killing of History: How a Discipline Is Being Murdered by Literary Critics and Social Theorists* (Sydney, 1994). For the impact of recent discussions on history teaching, see *National Standards for United States History for Grades K–4*, *National Standards for United States History for Grades 5–12*, and *National Standards for World History*, published in 1995 by the National Center for History in the Schools at the University of California at Los Angeles.

Index

Achard, Pierre, 92
Acton, Lord, 28
Adorno, Theodor, 12, 68, 70, 146, 147
Agulhon, Maurice, 62, 128, 129
Alltagsgeschichte, 105, 114, 115, 116
Althusser, Louis, 87, 89
American Historical Association, 28, 137
American Historical Review, 27–28, 135
Ankersmit, F. A., 11, 145
Annales, French historical journal, 3, 4, 51–64, 71, 82, 83, 84, 85, 87, 93, 107, 108, 112, 137–39
Appleby, Joyce, 174
Arendt, Hannah, 115
Ariès, Philippe, 60
Aristotle, 10
Ashton, T. S., 85
Auschwitz, 147

Bachelard, Gaston, 120
Bahners, Patrick, 119
Bakhtin, Mikhail, 83
Bancroft, George, 27
Barraclough, Geoffrey, 45
Barthes, Roland, 9, 10, 100, 118, 121, 126, 132, 135
Baudelaire, Charles, 142
Beard, Charles, 42
Becker, Carl, 42
Bell, Daniel, 6, 43, 98
Berkhofer, Robert, 10
Berlin, University of, 23–24
Berr, Henri, 5, 43
Bielefeld School, 69–70, 72, 76
Bielefeld, University of, 69–70, 71
Bismarck, Otto von, 29, 33, 36, 66
Blackbourn, David, 130

Blanc, Louis, 27
Bloch, Marc, 7, 52, 53, 54, 55–56, 57, 58, 59, 60, 62, 63, 82
Bourdieu, Paul, 11, 75, 125
Bouvier, Jean, 62
Braudel, Fernand, 7, 55, 56–57, 59, 63, 102
Breisach, Ernst, 174
Browning, Christopher, 115–16, 117
Brüggemeier, Franz-Josef, 74
Brunner, Otto, 128
Buckle, Henry Thomas, 79
Bujak, Franciszek, 82
Burckhardt, Jacob, 6, 7, 12, 118, 142
Burguière, André, 61
Burke, Edmund, 26
Burke, Peter, 103
Bury, John Bagnell, 34

Cambridge Group for the History of Population and Social Structure, 76
Chartier, Roger, 12, 140
Chartism, 130
Chaunu, Pierre, 60
Chevalier, Louis, 62
Childers, Thomas, 129–31, 135
CNRS (French National Council for Scientific Research), 55
Cobb, Richard, 87
Cobban, Alfred, 15, 85, 128–29
Collingwood, R. G., 127
Communist parties, 78, 81, 84
Communist Party's Historians Group (Great Britain), 84, 90
Comte, Auguste, 143
Condorcet, Jean Antoine, Marquis de, 40, 146
Conze, Werner, 73, 127–28